yes
you
can

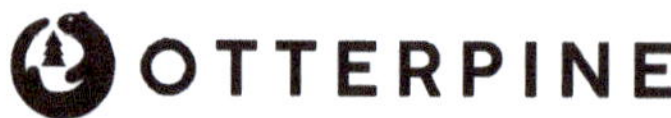

otterpine.com

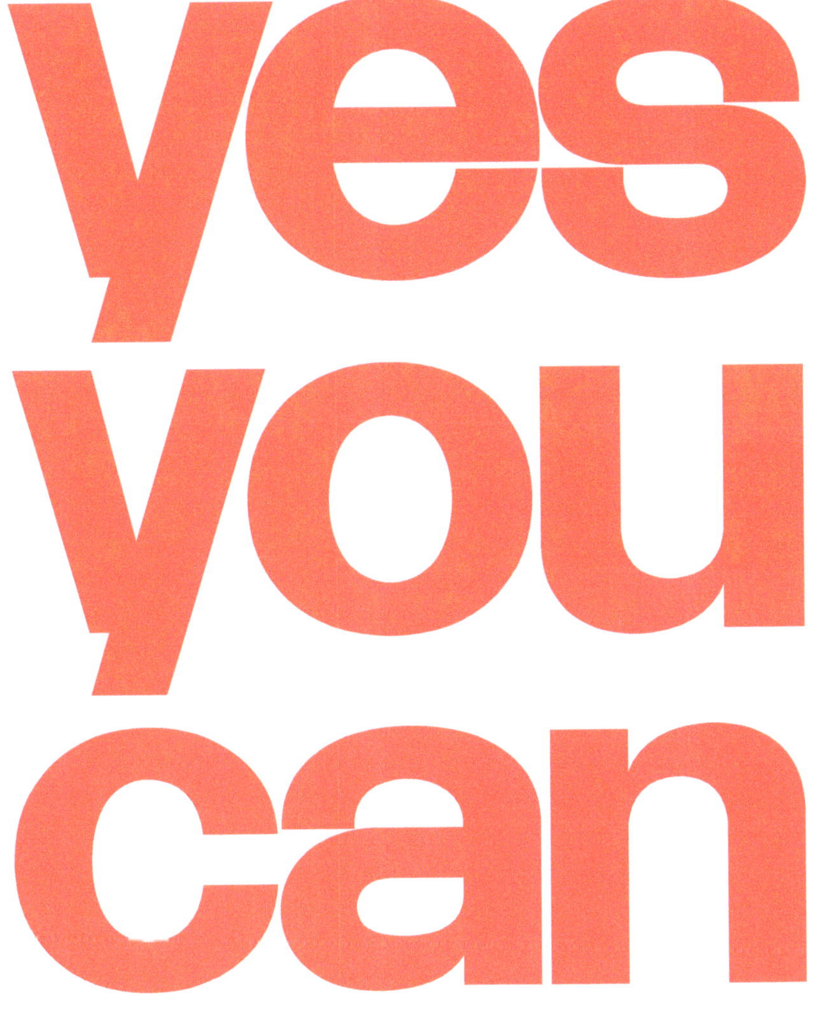

COURTNEY DANIELS
yes you can
HOW TO MAKE A MOVIE FOR ALMOST NO MONEY

*To the people I make movies with,
and to the people I watch movies with*

Contents

Introduction **3**

CHAPTER 1: The "Cheap Expensive" Route **11**

CHAPTER 2: The "Almost-No-Budget" Approach **35**

CHAPTER 3: Casting Your Project **49**

CHAPTER 4: The Script **65**

CHAPTER 5: Get a Camera…and Fall in Love **85**

CHAPTER 6: Lighting **125**

CHAPTER 7: Framing Shots and Getting Coverage **147**

CHAPTER 8: Getting Good Sound **161**

CHAPTER 9: Directing 175

CHAPTER 10: Production 195

CHAPTER 11: Post-Production 209

CHAPTER 12: Distribution—A Cautionary Tale 225

Conclusion: Yes You Can 237

Gear Shopping List 240

Suggested Reading List 242

Suggested Viewing List 244

References 246

About the Author 250

Introduction

In 1986, I was a freshman at the University of Texas at Austin. At that time, the Greek system had a big presence on campus and many students chose to join a sorority or fraternity. It was so common that if you were a middle-class kid like I was and you did not pursue it, some people would eye you skeptically and say, "So, you're a GDI, huh?" GDI stood for "goddamned independent."

Being a GDI was a more solitary path. Instead of immediately belonging to a big social group with many potential friends, you had to find like-minded people in a more organic way, which typically took more time.

When I came to Los Angeles in the '90s, my dream was to succeed in the Hollywood studio system. I had no intention of being a GDI. But after several years of writing spec script after spec script and getting nowhere, I finally decided to try to make films independently.

First, I made a short film called *The Jim Rapke Show*. It's a fictitious interview show in which the host, Jim Rapke, talks to bank customers who've participated in a "New Life Program," a bank offering in which customers pay a large sum of money to get a new career, house, and spouse. It was my first project with director of photography (DP) Dean Gunderson, and we shot the 14-page script in three days with a Panasonic DVX100. I spent only as much money as it took to pay Dean, a gaffer, a sound recordist, and an editor—somewhere between $2,000–3,000. The film screened at the LA Shorts International Film Festival in 2005.

After that, I wanted to make a feature, but I didn't have the money. So I spent weeks drawing up a formal business plan for making a slate of profitable low-budget films. My intent was to give the plan to wealthy investors, who I hoped would see me as a responsible, strategic partner with whom they could safely entrust hundreds of thousands of dollars. Note that this was before digital cameras had become really good and affordable. Most filmmakers were still shooting on film, which is more expensive than digital, and the accepted wisdom seemed to be that a typical independent film budget was around $1 million.[1] I planned to make each of my films for a fraction of that amount, even though I had no real idea of how to do that.

When I finished the 24-page business plan, which contained God only knows what, I realized I only knew three rich people I could give it to, and I was only comfortable approaching one of them. Actually, I didn't feel comfortable approaching him either, even though he is one of my favorite relatives. So I mailed the plan to him, was immediately mortified, then never had the courage to discuss it with him directly.

After I scrapped the business plan and despaired over never being able to make a film, it probably only took me two or three years to bounce back. That's when things got exciting. I had come up with a new plan: I was going to make a movie, not for a few hundred thousand dollars, but for *NO DOLLARS!*

When I announced this to my then-boyfriend-now-husband, Jimmy, he said, "Well...it's not going to cost NO money. It's going to cost *something*."

"Okay," I said. "I'll limit spending to $5,000."

"It's not going to be just $5,000," he countered.

"Okay, a little more than $5,000."

We continued like this until deciding on a budget around $15,000. (We ended up spending more than this. It's also worth noting that $15,000 in 2005 is worth about $22,000 in 2023.)

Around this time, I met my friend Stacie D'Amour for coffee in Burbank and told her my situation. Although I had briefly rallied, I was now feeling discouraged again.

---

1 I've since learned that many well-known filmmakers' first films cost nowhere near $1 million. Of course.

Stacie told me about a British film called *Abigail's Party*, made by Mike Leigh. She thought it would be inspiring.

I watched it and it blew my mind. It's a character-driven story that not only takes place in one location, but the camera appears to be locked off for most of the shoot. It was exactly what I needed at that moment. It convinced me that it's possible to make an interesting movie even with highly restrictive parameters.

I had already written a script that could be shot for a low budget, which I was calling "Untitled Married Couples Script." When my longtime friend Denise Donahoe told me there was a cool house in the Hollywood Hills where we could shoot for free, I jumped at the opportunity. We didn't know how long the house would be available, so we had to act quickly. We only had about four weeks of pre-production and spent most of it auditioning actors for the nine roles in the ensemble cast.

During the 13 days of shooting, everyone batted around possible names for the movie, and eventually, we landed on a title. The night after we wrapped, tired but relieved to have production behind us, Jimmy and I went to a bar to see actor Rob Smith, who plays "Dave" in the film, do standup comedy. When the emcee introduced Rob and said, "He was just in a movie called *What Other Couples Do*," I felt an internal shift. No more dreaming about making a movie. No more talking about making a movie. I had done it.

What Other Couples Do is about four LA couples who get together for a dinner party and decide to play Seven Minutes in Heaven. It has been streamed by over two million people.

Anyone can make a film, put it online, and potentially have it seen by thousands, maybe even millions of people, around the world. I want *you* to experience the thrill of getting a movie out there. If you're tired of dreaming and talking about it, I want to get you fired up to go for it. I hope that before you even get to the end of this book, you're already off and running.

In the coming chapters, I lay out two paths for making independent films affordably: a very lean version of the usual or traditional way—what I call the "cheap expensive" route—and the almost-no-budget route. I spend more time on the latter because it's my favorite. So, whether you have money for a "proper" shoot or you have just an iPhone, a boom mic, and a willingness to learn how to edit, by the end of this book, you'll know how to make a movie. It should be obvious by its length that this is not meant to be an exhaustively comprehensive guide. Instead my goal is to give you "just enough" information to get started. I recommend reading the book all the way through so that you're reasonably well-informed about the process of making a film, then you can return to chapters that require closer study.

In my opinion, when you make a super low-budget film, the win is not necessarily in getting pretty footage. The win is when you explore something the viewer can't turn away from. When you take them on a magic carpet ride through their own psyche. When you make them *feel* something.

Anyone who becomes great in their field probably spends as much time as possible doing what they love. They don't sit around talking about their limitations or waiting for help. All the filmmakers you admire? They didn't let anything stop them. Every one of them found a way to make their first film. And their second. And their third.

Wouldn't you like to be like them?

YOU CAN.

Chapter 1

The "Cheap Expensive" Route

Before we get into the "almost-no-budget" approach to filmmaking, let's cover what I call the "cheap expensive" route. If you have a tight, well-written script and can get your hands on $35,000, you could make your movie the usual or more traditional way. That is, you could team up with a talented DP (or a camera operator who wants to be a DP), hire a small crew, and work 10-hour days for about 12 days at a limited number of locations, ideally with a borrowed camera and a modest amount of gear.

You'll want to get an insurance policy to cover property damage and workers' comp, have a caterer deliver one hot meal per day, and reserve a portion of your funds for an editor, color correction, and an original score.

At this budget level, you probably won't be able to afford most of the usual or traditional comforts: a line producer and production staff, department heads, location managers, production assistants, a first assistant director (AD), script supervisor, set designer, prop department, shooting permits, etc. Two weeks of production will feel like two months. You'll be lucky to get five hours of sleep a night, and you'll be under tremendous stress the entire time. But working with a talented and skilled crew, no matter how small, can help ensure a quality execution of that rare and valuable thing—a great script.

Although I call it the expensive route, a budget of around $35,000 is ludicrously low to most people in Hollywood. In fact, many people spend this much to make a short film. But even if you can afford to spend more, it's not necessarily smart to do so. As filmmaker John Sayles has said, "The indie film business is not really a business." He compares it to a hobby—"like being a ski bum." Statistically, you're unlikely to get a distribution deal, and even if you do, you might not see much money from it. If you release your film on AVOD (advertising-based video on demand) streaming platforms with the help of an aggregator (an online company that helps DIY filmmakers with distribution), most pay only pennies per stream, sometimes less, and you have no idea if your movie will be seen by enough people to make a profit. Making a film is always an uncertain investment.

One scenario drastically changes the odds: if you have a direct connection to a star or a name actor (one whose name will move the needle) and can cast them in your movie, then you can justify spending more money on the film. If this is your situation, then you probably have access to other experienced people in the industry, in which case I'd suggest collecting informed opinions on what amount might be safe to invest.

If you're interested in the "around $35K" path to make a feature, here's an overview, followed by more detail.

Blueprint for Making a $35K Feature

Typically, you need a script that has been written specifically for a low-budget shoot. For example, one in which the story takes place in locations you can get for free and requires a limited number of actors (or a cast that agrees to a low pay rate). A low-budget script will usually not involve dolly shots, car chases, stunts, or special effects, and will usually be character-driven with captivating dialogue. Expect to spend around $25K on production (including the cast and crew's pay, a modest lighting package and gear rentals, an insurance policy, catering, and craft service). Expect to spend around $10K on post-production (including the editor's fee, color correction, the composer's fee, graphic design for the one-sheet, and LLC fees).

Pre-Production

As you might already be aware, production on a traditional shoot is essentially a race against the clock. Because each day of production is expensive (due to the cost of the cast and crew's pay, gear rentals, catering, etc.), the length of the shoot matters a lot. For a script of average length (90 to 105 pages), aim for around twelve days. To pull off shooting seven to nine pages a day, you'll have to be *really* on top of everything. If you're the producer and the director, it's possible you'll spend more time producing than directing during the actual shoot—which is why pre-production is so important.

The more you get done before the shoot, the more smoothly production will go and the more freed up you'll be to focus on directing during the shoot.

Try to allot at least six weeks for pre-production. If you have not yet found your cast, it's plausible you could spend the entire pre-production period auditioning actors, which is not ideal. In this case, try to give yourself more than six weeks for pre-production.

During pre-production, you should accomplish these tasks:

- Choose your (free) locations (houses, offices, shops, restaurants, bars, etc. that are owned by you, your family, your friends, or generous acquaintances)

- Create your shooting schedule and allocate your budget

- Hire a DP and sound recordist, plus any other crew you want and can afford

- Initiate contact with the Screen Actors Guild to be assigned a representative and start paperwork at least four weeks before production

- Decide whether you want to hire a payroll company to handle pay for cast and crew; find out whether your state requires you to pay "fringes" (fringe benefits) and take this into account when calculating the pay rate you can afford to offer cast and crew

- Rent a camera (if your DP can't borrow one from a friend, or from school if they're a student) as well as a modest lighting package and gear

- Buy an insurance policy (SAG requires it and so do gear rental houses, at least for certain equipment)

- Find an editor

- Create a shot list

- Block scenes with your DP (and actors, if possible)

- Find a caterer

- Decide the cast's hair and makeup looks and collect the wardrobe for each actor

- Collect items for set decor

- Collect all the props called for in the script

- Identify where cast and crew will park at the shooting location(s)

- Find out if there will be construction crews competing for parking and creating noise in the vicinity of your shooting location(s) during your planned production period

Scheduling the Shoot

Your start date and schedule will most likely be determined by the availability of your shooting locations, DP, and lead actors. Aside from these parameters, try to shoot scenes in the order they take place in your script, to whatever extent you can (this may not be entirely possible if you have multiple locations). That way, as you build to the climax of the story, you can assess how everything is adding up and decide whether you need to write any additional scenes or dialogue to clarify anything. This will also help you gauge how emotional the actors' performances should be.

If you want to learn the most professional, efficient, and elegant way to break down a script and schedule a shoot, read Ralph S. Singleton's classic, *Film Scheduling*. It's an interesting, informative, and helpful book.

Scheduling a shoot can also be accomplished by just using common sense and organizational skills. If you have 100 pages to shoot and only 12 days of production, and you know that realistically you can "only" shoot seven to nine pages a day, then you can simply divide your script into seven-to-nine-page chunks and assign each chunk to one day of shooting. If you're not married to the idea of shooting your script in order and want to be as efficient as possible, you can plan to shoot all scenes that occur in one location (say, all the kitchen scenes, or all the bedroom scenes) one after the other, grouping those that require similar lighting setups. This will reduce transition times.

You'll definitely want to avoid unnecessary "company moves" (a location change). You should plan to shoot all the scenes that occur in a location in one stay rather than having to return to the location. Because it takes time for a crew to break down gear, load out, and then load in to a new location, you might have to do a thorough cleaning more than once or hire a housekeeping crew to do it, etc.

It's smart to have a plan B for each day of shooting, in case of inclement weather or an actor's unavailability. Especially if you shoot in LA, often during indie film shoots, actors will suddenly become unavailable for a portion of a day. This is because most prioritize studio projects and sometimes they will get an audition or callback for a TV show or film. When this happens, you just quickly look for other scenes you can shoot. Call the actor(s) needed for those scenes to see if they're available on short notice, and try to keep getting footage in the can.

If organizational skills are not your strong suit, you might want to hire a newish (i.e., affordable) line producer who's looking to get more experience or credits. You'll likely have to make budget cuts elsewhere in order to afford one. Or you could try recruiting a very organized friend or family member with whom you get along well and who is willing to work for cheap.

Hiring Crew

There are pros and cons to having a bigger crew vs. a skeleton crew. Having a bigger crew should mean a reduction of the tasks you're responsible for, freeing you up to focus on directing. But keep in mind that a small crew usually stays busier and moves faster than a big crew. Also, each person you hire represents another personality to deal with, another mouth to feed, and another parking space needed at the shooting location(s). To find crew (and cast), Mandy.com is a good resource.

Depending on how ambitious your shoot is, you might be able to get away with what some would argue is the only crew you need: a DP and a sound recordist. The argument for hiring additional crew for the DP is that it will likely speed up the time it takes for each lighting setup. Having crew enables the DP to stay behind the camera to see the effect of tweaks made to the lighting by the crew (rather than the DP having to keep going back and forth between the lighting setup and camera/monitor). Your DP might want any number of the following: a camera assistant, focus puller, grip, gaffer, and one or two swing people.

In LA, expect to pay a DP (or camera operator who wants to build up their DP reel) around $250/day. To me, the ideal is to partner with a DP or camera operator who is willing to work for deferred pay in the form of a flat fee, ongoing royalties from percentage points in the film, or a mutually agreed upon rate for production plus a percentage of royalties. If you go the royalties route, you will likely want to stipulate that they'll begin receiving their share after you've recouped the cost of making the film. I partnered with DP Dean Gunderson on *What Other Couples Do*, and with DP Bianca Butti on my second movie, *Bedroom Story*, and both were great collaborators. Each helped me stay within budget, they both have good taste and are a pleasure to work with, and they made my movies look beautiful.

Ideally, your DP will own or be able to borrow a good camera for the shoot, saving you the cost of renting one. If not, BorrowLenses.com offers affordable rates and they FedEx cameras (as well as other gear) directly to you. I've had nothing but great experiences with them.

Expect to pay at least $150-200/day or more per person for other camera crew. At this low rate, you might have to hire inexperienced people, such as film school students who are eager to start building a reel. If your script is really strong, or if you or your DP are well-connected, you might be able to attract experienced people who'll accept less than their usual day rate. For comparison's sake: a really good, experienced gaffer might bring all their own gear and charge as much as $750/day. Together, you and your DP should decide your priorities and how much you can stretch or cut corners elsewhere.

One approach for paying a DP and crew is to offer everyone the same rate and be transparent about it. This way, everyone knows they're valued equally and no one is left wondering whether they're being paid less than the next person.

If you care about what kind of personalities you'll be dealing with on set—and trust me, you will—tell your DP you'd like to be involved in the hiring of the crew (as opposed to leaving it entirely to them). Start a list of names and contact info for possible backup crew who can be called upon if/when someone doesn't show up to set.

At the under-$40K budget level, you won't be able to afford a line producer, first AD, and script supervisor without making painful cuts elsewhere. However, if you can find a way to get quality people for a very affordable rate for any of these positions, it will make production smoother. I've not yet had a line producer or script supervisor on my projects, but I look forward to experiencing the luxury of hiring these key people on future projects.

Expect to distribute paychecks daily for crew who are only working for one day and weekly for those who are staying the entire production.

Getting Good Sound is Critical

Good sound is even more important than picture quality. In fact, it's been said that "people don't watch a movie, they listen to a movie." Think about it: If the sound quality of a movie sucks (if there's crackling, or an annoying hum, or if you can't make out the dialogue), you quickly stop caring whether the cinematography is good. Whereas if the sound is pristine, you'll probably tolerate a grainy or overexposed picture.

Expect to pay $400/day or more for a sound recordist, who will bring with them all the gear needed for recording both boom mic and lavalier mic sound. You might also have to provide extra money every other day to cover battery costs for their gear. (You'd be amazed how many batteries are required and how quickly they're depleted. The AAA batteries that sit in your tv remote control for two years are done after a day or two on set.)

Alternatively, you could buy boom mic recording gear (such as a Zoom brand F1-SP field recorder with a shotgun mic for around $229, a Rode brand telescopic boom pole for $49, and any needed accessories such as a shock mount and a small 3/8"-16 female threaded adapter to 1/4"-20 male threaded post for attaching the recorder to the pole) and pay a friend or family member a mutually agreeable rate to record sound. If so, be sure to have them watch tutorials online for getting good boom mic sound, have them practice using the boom pole and field recorder, and ask them to make a few test recordings in different conditions (indoors, outdoors, with one person speaking, and with multiple people speaking) for you, and ideally also for your editor, to make sure they have attained competency. It would be ideal to also buy a couple of $200 Sennheiser lavalier microphones and a couple of 100-count packages of Rycote stickies so that the actors can be "lav mic-ed" for every scene as well. Boom mic sound is the gold standard—a boom mic picks up ambient sound, making for richer, more true-to-life audio—but lav mic sound is valuable backup for your editor to have as well. All the sound gear will require batteries, so make sure you buy a good stock of AA or AAA batteries, whichever are needed.

A professional sound recordist will do this automatically, but be sure to tell an inexperienced sound recordist to record at least one minute of room tone immediately prior to or following every scene you shoot. Also, make sure a nonprofessional sound recordist knows that they must set the gain level on the field recorder each time they record. You can read a lot more about gain and room tone in Chapter 8: Getting Good Sound.

When recording with a boom, it's best to have the mic positioned a few inches in front of the actor's face and pointed down at a diagonal to the middle of their chin. The closer the mic is to the actor, the better the sound. Rather than leaving the mic in the same position to capture two actors' dialogue, it's better to turn the mic toward whomever is speaking.

Finally, keep in mind that, with sound recording, an ounce of prevention is worth a pound of cure. It is WAY better to make every effort to get good sound during the shoot rather than count on fixing it in post! Often, bad sound can be made better, but it can't always be made *good*. So it's key to have your sound recordist constantly checking to make sure they're getting good sound during each day's shoot. Part of their job on set will be to tell you if the sound on a take is usable or if there was something (an airplane, helicopter, bus, car horn, etc.) that will make the take unusable. They'll need a set of headphones and they'll need to feel completely comfortable using the playback controls on the field recorder.

Gear Rentals

Your DP will know what they need to light the movie, but plan to rent only a modest lighting package and minimal gear (spending around $1,000 for a two-week shoot). If you or your DP really want a dolly shot, plan to rent the gear for just one day. If you're able to work on a weekend, you can pay for just a "one day" rental—a Friday—but you'll have the gear for two extra days, as most production houses are not open on the weekend (you'd return the gear on Monday). You have to show proof of insurance at gear rental houses, and some might only take cashier's checks—find out their policies on this *before* you drive over to pick up the gear. Also, dollies are incredibly heavy, so you'll need to take a couple of strong people with you to help you put one in your truck or van. Your DP might also ask you to get some expendables, like Visqueen (to cover windows, when shooting day for night).

The Cast

If you don't already have actors in mind for your project and don't know how to find actors, read Chapter 3: Casting Your Project. If you already have your cast—say, two lead actors and a handful of supporting actors—consider offering a flat rate to each lead, depending on what you can afford and what they'll accept, and $125/day or more to the supporting actors. Plan to shoot all the supporting actors' scenes in one day, if possible.

If you are working with much less than $35K, you can discuss with your actors whether they're willing to accept deferred pay, in which case they'll receive a mutually agreed upon fee after the movie has been released and is in the black. If so, print a boilerplate contract from the net or download a film production forms app on your phone and collect signatures from your cast before production begins. However, I've been told by actor friends that they prefer to be paid during production. They say it's not as much about the money as it is about being respected as a working actor. So, if you can possibly pay your cast at the time of production, it's best to do so.

If you cast actors who are in the Screen Actors Guild, making your movie a SAG production will require you to contribute a certain percentage, on top of the actors' wages, to the actors' health and medical benefits and pensions. This also shows respect for actors, without whom you could not make your movie. Call or contact SAG early—at least four weeks before your production start date—to get assigned a representative who will be your contact throughout the production process. Start a folder on your computer for collecting documents from SAG, and dedicate a binder (physical, not digital) to hold forms that will need to be signed daily by the actors when they clock in and out on set.

Locations

On a $35K budget, you can usually only afford to shoot at free locations. This might mean asking friends or family to let you shoot at their homes, in their cars, or at their offices or other places of business. If someone grants you permission, you'll want to make every effort to protect their property. But no matter how hard you try, there will be at least some minor dings or scratches. So be honest with yourself and your friends or family—if they are uptight and will never forgive you, don't shoot at their place. To me, the ideal is to shoot in your own home, your own backyard, your own car, on your own driveway, etc. That way, if anything is scratched, dented or destroyed, it's your problem—only you have to live with the consequences—and you won't have to pay who knows how much to replace or repair someone else's property (and your relationship with them).

If you decide you must pay for a desired location, know that you're going to have to make painful sacrifices elsewhere in your budget. In LA (and even other big cities), most homeowners, storekeepers, etc. know they can charge high fees for renting their location to movie companies and ad agencies for commercial shoots.

Although it can make your life easier to shoot in just one location, an upside to changing locations break pro-duction to close gap is that it gives everyone fresh energy.

Find out if your locations have good cell phone reception. If they don't, plan how you'll communicate with cast and crew (consider walkie-talkies). Also, find out whether the electrical wiring for any residential location is outdated or insufficient for the gear that will need to be powered during production. You may need to hire an electrician for a couple of hours to find out.

Insurance Coverage

Buy insurance to protect yourself, your cast and crew, the gear, and the property you shoot on. On my films, I've paid around $3,000 for workers' comp insurance, equipment insurance, and third-party property insurance. Know that it'll be more expensive if your shoot involves variables that add unpredictability and possible danger, such as animals, shooting on a body of water, etc.

Script Fee

If you have written the script yourself, decide whether you want to receive a script fee to be paid to you once the film is in the black. Decide what you think is a fair and reasonable amount and obtain written agreement from your producing partners.

Props

Go through the script, highlighting all the props that will be needed. Collect them and store them in bags or bins labeled with the scenes in which they'll be used. If you neglect to do this, you'll be racing around collecting items during production, which is a waste of valuable time.

Wardrobe, Hair, and Makeup

Go through the script to identify how many changes of wardrobe there will be for each character. Then get with the actors to choose their wardrobe from their own clothing or other available clothing, such as yours or your producing partners'. (My husband, Jimmy, often notices his shirts on actors in my movies!) Shoot short wardrobe, hair, and makeup tests to make sure you like how each actor's planned looks appear on camera and to see if there are any issues with the fit and functionality of their clothing.

If you have an ensemble cast, you'll likely need two hair and makeup people in order to have all the actors ready in time to shoot, especially on days when you're shooting group scenes. Sometimes special makeup or hair products are needed for individual actors. Find out early.

Set Decor

Choose set decor items from your own home or other free, available resources such as family or friends who are willing to let you "shop" their homes. Be prepared to pay the replacement value of anything that gets damaged, taken, or lost during production. No, really—be prepared for this possibility!

Floor Protection

Buy a roll of carpet protection tape (from Uline or other supplier) or wood floor protective film (from ArmorDillo or other brand) for the location house(s), since C-stands and other gear can dent or scratch flooring.

Music

Expect to pay a composer somewhere around $1,200 for an original score. Hiring a music supervisor and paying licensing fees to a variety of bands is fantastic if you can afford it! Keep in mind that even if you contact a band directly and have a good rapport, you usually end up having to do business with their manager or music rights publisher, paying whatever fee they ask. It is usually simpler and more affordable to work with one composer, and it can be a very rewarding collaboration.

Color Correction

Your DP will likely insist on having the movie color corrected, and you'll probably be eager to do it—it usually makes a big difference in how good your finished film looks. In the past, I've spent around $3,000 for color correction, but you may be able to get it done for less now. If spending this kind of money is unthinkable, and if your DP agrees to it, you could ask your editor if they're game to consider doing the color correction themselves, using a LUT (short for Lookup Table—a preset color look that can be applied to an entire movie at once, for fast color correction) and other increasingly more sophisticated tools available in Adobe Premiere Pro or other editing programs. Typically, a DP will sit in on the first session with the colorist or editor to tell them how they want the movie to look (for example, how saturated they want the color to be, etc.).

Catering and Craft Service

In addition to hiring a caterer to serve one hot meal per day, you'll want to pay them to provide coffee service. If you don't provide coffee from morning until night, your cast will leave set to get it. You'll have to find someone very reasonable in order to be able to afford catering, but it's critical because an army travels on its stomach. You must provide at least one hot, good meal per day. It's also nice to provide breakfast if there's an early call time, and you might want to order some pizzas for everyone to snack on while finishing a late night. Crews that typically work on professional shoots expect to be fed at certain intervals because they are used to union jobs. Like my mom—a Southerner—says about wedding receptions: "Never keep people waiting for food." Always have something out and available for people to graze on. Craft service can be packaged snacks as well as some fresh fruit.

Unless you've polled your entire cast and crew, do not assume everyone prefers to eat healthy. It's key to include some stick-to-the-ribs options (think meat and starchy carbs) for heartier eaters who will not appreciate salads. Production is usually grueling and people need good food, as well as caffeine and sugar, to get through it.

I strongly recommend you don't buy pallets of bottled water. What happens is everyone opens a bottle, takes two sips, then leaves it somewhere on the property where you're shooting. Not only is it incredibly wasteful, *you* will endlessly be collecting half-full plastic bottles and stray caps as you struggle to keep the set relatively tidy. Instead, ask everyone to bring a refillable, reusable water bottle to set, or consider providing personalized water bottles at the start of production to ensure everyone has their own readily identifiable bottle. If you must buy pallets of plastic-bottled water, consider providing Sharpies so that everyone can write their name on a bottle each time they open one. Even if this doesn't stop everyone from wasting water, at least when you're going around collecting half-full water bottles, you'll know who needs to be reined in.

Cast and Crew Parking

Know what your plan is for having cast and crew park their cars when they arrive at the shooting location(s). You do not want to risk disturbing neighbors and getting shut down. If you have a big cast and crew (say, 25 people), consider having everyone meet off site and carpool to the set OR hire a driver to ferry everyone back and forth to parking. It's not ideal, but I know from personal experience that it's not practical to have everyone park blocks away and walk to set.

The Editor

Expect to pay your editor $3,000 or more. If they're good, they're worth every penny. Second to you (or the line producer, if you spring for one), they'll probably log the most hours on your film. And a great editor can radically improve a film, making a hot mess watchable and making a good film even better. Start looking for an editor during pre-production. Good ones are usually busy on higher profile projects. If you attract one that is excited about your project, cherish them. The ideal is to hire them before you begin production. If they can begin transferring dailies to their computer starting on Day 1 of production, all the better. If so, you'll have to arrange how they're going to get the dailies (after you transfer each day's footage to hard drives).

Titles and Poster Design

Expect to pay $300 or more for titles (opening and end credits) from a freelance designer. If you have no money for title design, you can supply your editor with a typed list of credits (being sure to have the correct spelling of each person's name, of course) so that they can create simple opening and end credits.

Expect to pay $300 or more for professional graphic design of the one-sheet (the movie poster) in various sizes (landscape and portrait) to meet asset requirements for Filmhub or another aggregator.

The key art for a movie is very important and must be compelling even when viewed at thumbnail-size on a phone screen, such as on apps like Just Watch. For this reason, it can be very helpful to have a photographer visit your set and shoot some stills that might be used in the poster design. After each project, I have experienced major regret over not asking a talented friend to come shoot stills.

Whether you handle the poster design yourself or hire a graphic designer, when choosing a font(s) for the title of your movie, you might want to go with one that is unique, as opposed to the ones we all see every day (i.e., the fonts available for free in Microsoft Word and in Google Docs). Choosing an overly familiar "basic" font can telegraph that the project is amateurish and make viewers less likely to take a chance on it.

Form an LLC

It costs around $70 to form an LLC for a production, as a legal precaution to protect yourself, plus an $800 state fee (in California; this may differ in other states) each year to maintain it. The state fees really add up over the years (for example, seven years of keeping an LLC = $5,600), so you might want to talk to a lawyer to get their advice on how long you should keep it. I think there's no right answer. It

just depends on your budget or comfort level (how safe
you like to play things).

Festival Fees

Film festivals typically charge between $40-100 for entry
fees, depending on if you're submitting by their early,
regular, or late deadline. Don't underestimate how much
it'll cost to enter a ton of festivals. I spent around $3,000
in festival entrance fees for my first movie.

File Storage

You'll need to purchase several hard drives big enough to
store all your footage: one to download the dailies to; one
for backup of the raw footage; one to go back and forth
between the editor and you each day, so the editor can
transfer each day's footage to their editing system; and at
least one more for backup on which to save the final draft
of the film.

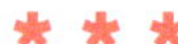

Well, that's about it.

I know what you're thinking: "What?! I need more info!
More, more, more!" Right? "And throw in a steady IV drip of
reassurance!"

But look, you've got enough info to get started. So, go
ahead! Start assembling your team, planning your budget,
and scheduling your shoot. DOOOO IT!

Okay, fine. Maybe you're not feeling quite ready yet.
So keep reading to learn about the "almost-no-budget"

approach, which contains plenty of tips that will be helpful even if you do have some money.

But then you gotta get down to business!

Chapter 2

The "Almost-No-Budget" Approach

After finishing post-production on *What Other Couples Do* (and still a few years away from making back the money we'd invested in it), I wasn't immediately ready to make another movie. Making *WOCD* was intense. To me, making a super-low-budget movie the proper way is like making a cross-country road trip. After you do it, you need time to recover before it starts to seem like a fun idea again.

The Need for a More Sustainable Approach

Even though I prefer movies to any other type of entertainment, I started thinking about making something shorter and easier to execute than a feature. Having lived in LA for almost two decades at that point, I wanted to write about what it's like to try to succeed here. So I began working on a half-hour pilot called *This Fucking Town*.

When I finished the script, I of course wanted to shoot it. And I thought production would be less painful if I worked smaller this time, with just a DP and sound recordist. For reasons I don't remember, we split the shoot into two chunks (I think because there was a party scene and I wanted adequate time to prepare for it). What was supposed to be just a short break between the shoots became a few months, probably due to a combination of scheduling conflicts and inertia. (In indie filmmaking, it often takes a big burst of energy to get everything up and moving again.)

Once we finally had all the footage in the can, it took several months to finish post. In part because my editor, who is not only fantastically talented but also an absolute pleasure to collaborate with, is always in demand. At that point, he was on a big studio film and was working long hours, including every weekend.

All in all, it took almost a year to make a 14-minute pilot. During that time, I became frustrated by the process. Originally, I had been thinking I would make a whole series. But now I was dreading the slog. My script for episode two was ready to go, but I couldn't bring myself to plan the shoot.

Discouraged and depressed, I felt like I was at a crossroads.

One day, while scribbling thoughts on a notepad, I suddenly found myself listing all the reasons I had come to dislike production:

1. Hiring professional, experienced crew on a super tight budget is stressful. I always feel like I'm in over my head. Even if I'm paying industry-average wages, I feel like it's not enough. It's not the crew's dream to make your project, it's your dream. For the crew, it's a *job*, and they take pride in doing it well. I always wish I could pay more, not to mention provide more of the creature comforts that would make the day-to-day grind of production more pleasant. Not being able to do these things is stress-producing.

2. Continuing to self-finance proper shoots (i.e., with a crew) is not sustainable.

3. To make any project, even a modest one, I am dependent on a group of people.

4. Because talented people are often already booked and working on high-profile, higher-priority projects, I'm often in a holding pattern, waiting until they have free time to work on mine.

5. Getting great lighting takes time. Setting up a shot often takes over an hour. And I write dialogue-heavy scenes. Usually, by the time we finally begin shooting, I can only get a few takes. Because if I want to stay on schedule, I have to move on quickly so the crew can start setting up the next shot.

Seeing these things on paper gave me clarity.

I don't doubt production can be a blast when you have a nice-sized budget and your project is everyone's top priority. But it was liberating just to acknowledge that working with a group at my budget level was rough. And though I could justify spending the money we did on my first movie, it felt unwise to spend more money on this project when I didn't even know yet whether I would recoup what we spent on the movie.

As I thought about these things, it started to dawn on me that if I wanted to shoot more episodes of my series, maybe great cinematography, professional sound, and a wonderful editor were luxuries I couldn't afford. This realization felt like a breakthrough.

I started to wonder if I could free myself from doing things the traditional way.

What if I could work more affordably and therefore be able to make more stuff?

What if I could spend more time with the actors and had the luxury of getting more takes?

What if I could eliminate the pressure that typically comes with being on set?

What if I could travel light and move quickly?

What if I could do everything myself?

This last thought scared the hell out of me. But I was desperate enough to try.

A Super Indie Path

In the mid-to-late '90s, I read Robert Rodriguez's *Rebel Without a Crew* and loved it. But I thought the only reason a person would make a movie on their own is because they had no choice. It never occurred to me that shooting solo in the almost-no-budget range would be a fun, rewarding way to work.

But in between making two features (the second one, *Bedroom Story*, with just a DP, gaffer, sound recordist, and my husband Jimmy) and the pilot for *This Fucking Town*, I shot more material for episodes 1, 2, 3, and 4 of *This Fucking Town* on my own. And it was a fantastic experience. Low pressure and low stakes! Working alone with the actors was intimate and fun, and it allowed for greater connection.

I can't emphasize enough how different an experience it is to work alone compared to a typical shoot. You can shoot for a few hours a day, a few days a week, have balance in your life, and actually enjoy the process.

When I first started shooting alone, I told myself *This Fucking Town* would be my training ground. I knew I would make a lot of mistakes and I decided to just make peace with that. Because I was learning so many new skills and juggling so many tasks alone, my approach to lighting was based on expediency. I supplemented available light and practicals with use of one broad diffused lighting source (a dimmable LED panel). It took a while to figure out how to get good sound, but if you look at my camera work in the episodes, though it's not showy, it's solid. I got good angles, everything's in focus, and the footage cuts together. Most importantly, the story tracks and the actors' performances are great. And audience feedback has been enthusiastic so far. In fact, *This Fucking Town* might be my most popular project.

Somewhere along the way, I realized the episodes could be shoved together to make a movie. This fascinated me. The idea that one person could shoot a series or feature alone, working with just their cast, blew my mind. I came away from it wanting to shoot more projects this way. And I want to urge other people to consider it, too—which is why I'm writing this book.

Clearly, people need more encouragement to think outside the Hollywood paradigm, because too many would-be filmmakers are still sitting on the sidelines, waiting to be picked by one of the big studios or streamers. Or they're waiting to get financing some other way. Even in LA, this is common—maybe especially in LA, where it's just expected that you'll have a traditional shoot, requiring a lot of money.

But enough preamble. Let's talk about how YOU can make a feature or series—without waiting for financing!

When to Shoot Solo

There are many scenarios in which the almost-no-budget route of shooting solo (working with just your cast) is ideal. For example, if/when:

- You simply don't have the money for a shoot

- You're concerned about the odds of recouping or making a return on your investment

- You suspect your script is not commercial or might not appeal to a sizable niche audience

- You don't know if your script is strong enough to warrant spending $35,000 or more to execute it

- You don't want to be dependent on a group of people to make something

- You think a down-and-dirty execution of your script could be cool, aesthetically and otherwise

- You would like to be able to experiment—explore different storyline possibilities, let actors improvise, etc.—without worrying whether you'll end up with a commercially viable film

- You want to make other types of video projects (such as branding videos, tutorials, music videos, marketing or promotional videos) and don't want to spend thousands on them

- You have experience making films or other types of videos with a group of people but have been wanting a more sustainable path forward

- You want to experience the joy of shooting more often, without having to schedule and wait for a big, expensive shoot

When to Find a Collaborator

"She was gnarly and extreme—my idea of the collaborator I hoped to find at film school."

— CINEMATOGRAPHER JOSHUA JAMES RICHARDS TALKING ABOUT DIRECTOR CHLOE ZHAO

For some people, working solo and not needing to rely on others is a dream. For others, it's a lonely path. If you don't want to do everything on your own, find a friend who has skills and talents that complement yours.

If you're eager to operate the camera and light scenes but you don't know what to shoot, team up with an "idea person," a good improviser, or a writer. If you're a writer who wants to direct, team up with a friend who is into learning about the camera and lighting.

You don't need to partner with someone who's brilliant. You need to partner with someone who you enjoy spending time with, who is available, and who is eager to make stuff.

YOUR "Almost-No-Budget" Approach

Whatever amount of money you've got, here's what you're going to do with it: You're going to buy a camera and some gear and you're going to learn how to do everything your-self: operate the camera, light the actors, record sound, and edit the footage.

Yes, it IS possible. *Even if you currently know nothing about any of this.*

I know, because I used to be a person who couldn't even set the time/date buttons on a wristwatch.[2] In fact, when I rented a camera from BorrowLenses.com for the pilot shoot of *This Fucking Town*, I opened the box it was shipped in, gingerly lifted the camera out and handed it directly to my DP. I was completely intimidated by it.

But a year later, when I was frustrated and ready, I bought that same camera for myself, as well as a subscription to Adobe Premiere Pro editing software. Within three months, I had learned just enough to start shooting and editing scenes for *This Fucking Town*.

Think about that. Within three months, YOU could be shooting and editing footage. Isn't that wild?

---

2 I often tell the story of how, when I was 27 years old, I watched my much younger sister, who was eight at the time, sit down with a new digital watch and immediately begin figuring out how to set it and use all of the features. I couldn't believe it. The secret to learning technical stuff is to not be afraid and just dive in.

Sure, instead of charting your own DIY course, you could spend two or three years in film school.[3] But why would you want to? Why not go all in on learning only what you really need to, fast, so that you can start making your first film?

Will your movie win cinematography awards? Not likely. Will the sound be decent? If you're very careful, yes. Will you learn a ton? I guarantee it. Will you make something that's perfectly imperfect and has flashes of brilliance, that your friends and family will love? Hell yeah!

But here's the best part: When you own the means of production and know how to do everything yourself, *there's nothing stopping you from making more projects.* Which means you'll keep learning and getting better, which will give you confidence—which is huge! Because buried under all the fake obstacles is the real one: fear.

In fact, if you're feeling freaked out right now, just take a deep breath. If you can't even imagine doing everything yourself and are not at all sure you want to attempt it, *you don't have to decide yet*. There's a lot of ground to cover first. Just read the coming chapters and let everything incubate.

Let it *fester*.

Because it will. And maybe, by the end of this book, you'll be ready to go for it.

So, c'mon, let's do this. If you already have a script that's tailored to a super-low-budget shoot and you've already offered roles to actors or friends or family, skip ahead to Chapter 5: Get a Camera...and Fall in Love. Otherwise, keep reading.

---

3 If you think it's necessary to attend film school to learn technical skills or develop a point of view or style, consider the list of directors who did not attend film school: Akira Kurosawa, Alfred Hitchcock, Stanley Kubrick, Quentin Tarantino, Mike Nichols, Nora Ephron, Ava DuVernay, Julie Taymor, Catherine Hardwicke, Terry Gilliam, Harold Ramis, Wes Craven, Wes Anderson, James Cameron, Lilly and Lana Wachowski, and David Fincher, among others.

Chapter 3

Casting Your Project

Drawing up a list of people you'd like to cast before you write a script might seem like putting the cart before the horse. But I think it's smart to keep in mind the most charismatic or interesting people in your available talent pool as you write your script. In fact, if you're acquainted with someone who is particularly talented or compelling to watch, make them your muse. Come up with a story that can be centered around them.

Your potential cast list should include anyone you know personally or have easy access to, specifically friends, family, and acquaintances who you think are likable, charming, interesting to watch, or who otherwise possess some kind of appeal.

Also, list anyone in your local community who you find compelling and could easily approach (for example: waiters, bartenders, yoga instructors, personal trainers, etc.), as well as what the industry calls "unknown actors" (aspiring actors or working actors that are not widely known) who you've seen in local plays or other performances.

The ideal is to work with people who not only have a compelling presence onscreen but who are also pleasant to be around. And they must be willing and able to allocate time to shooting. After the novelty of making a movie wears off, you don't want to be begging your actors for time.

Holding Out for Stars

If you're thinking of ignoring the above advice because you're fantasizing about casting stars or name actors, please consider this: It is nearly impossible to attach known actors to a project if you are an unknown director working with a very small budget.

How do I know? Because I've tried. I've DM-ed stars on Instagram, I've approached them in comedy clubs, I've handed them scripts at health food restaurants—I've done everything you can think of. And what they all say is that they can't accept a script from you for legal reasons. Which is of course understandable.

But I did once go through the proper channels. Here's what happened:

For my movie *Bedroom Story*, I asked a respected casting director if she could help me get a star for the lead female role. I wanted someone around 50 years old, and since you always hear that there are fewer opportunities for older actresses, and since famous actresses are always saying there should be more women directors, I thought there was a chance we might attract someone.

But the casting director told me that unless I had just recently won the Palme d'Or at Cannes it would be very difficult to get a star. I said, "How difficult?" She said, "Like, peel-your-face-off-the-wall impossible." I said, "Okay, let's try."

So, I paid her $3,500 (half of her usual fee; she was nice enough to give me a deal) and she sent my script to the agents or managers of six or seven famous actresses.

Each time she submitted my script, she told the agent or manager the thoughtfully crafted pitch we'd come up with, in hopes of inspiring them to support our quest. After waiting an average of a couple of weeks or more for each star to read the script, each of the reps told us they were passing on my project.

It was demoralizing to keep getting no's, and the process took months. And I was out $3,500.

Yes, it might have made a difference if I had made a cash offer to the actresses. But no one could tell me what amount would make them seriously consider the project. $50,000? $100,000? More? Much, much more? Even if I'd known what amount to offer, it's possible I wouldn't have been able to borrow or raise it. And yes, it's likely that the actresses' reps discouraged them from working on a small independent film, or didn't even tell them about my project, since I hadn't made a cash offer.

But I learned something important from the experience. What did I learn? Fuck trying to get stars attached.

Find Your Own Stars

Instead of being bummed about not being able to cast a star, why not get excited about the possibility of discovering new talent? Think of it as a fun challenge: Are you convinced you have a good eye? Prove it! Pick an actor with breakout potential.

I still remember how exciting it was to witness newcomer Connie Britton's performance in Ed Burns' first movie, *The Brothers McMullen*. Maybe your niece will charm audiences like Abigail Breslin did in *Little Miss Sunshine*. Maybe the charismatic guy at your local FedEx store is the next Seth Rogen.

Holding Out for the "Perfect" Unknown Actor

After trying to attach a star to *Bedroom Story*, I dragged my feet for another year or more before shooting it, because none of the actors who were available to me were exactly right for the lead role. As I said, I wanted someone who was around 50 years old.

Now, when I look back, it kills me that I wasted so much time stressing about casting someone who was the perfect age. Yes, casting is important. But making a movie and getting on with your life is important, too.

If you know a great actor and they're not the right age—or they are somehow not what you envisioned for the role—really think about how important your criteria are. *Question your assumptions.*

I knew my frequent collaborator Annie Cavalero was a great actor and a joy to work with. But I kept getting tripped up by her young age. I assumed I had to cast an actress who was at least over 40. I should have questioned this assumption sooner than I did.

This might be unthinkable to the writers out there, but even if you have to change something fundamental about your script/story to make it right for your actor, DO IT. Don't be precious about your writing. When I finally bit the bullet and revised my script to accommodate Annie's age, it was a relief and thrill to offer her the role and move forward.

Find Someone Who's Already the Character

One way to approach casting is to find an actor who innately has the main quality called for in a role. Someone who exudes the traits you want, without acting. This way, you're not holding your breath, hoping they can be what you need them to be. They're already the character—24/7!

Where to Find Actors

In LA, you can meet actors virtually anywhere and every-where. At showcases; local theater productions; Upright Citizens Brigade and the Groundlings sketch comedy shows; and on the staff of nearly every yoga studio, Pilates studio, gym, restaurant, bar, and coffee shop. But if you're not in LA, there are plenty of options for finding actors:

- Post casting calls and search for talent at CastingFrontier.com and Backstage.com.

- Search the websites of casting agents and talent agents who are based in your own city. Most feature the headshots of clients, along with a search engine that allows you to filter for age and type.

- Every casting agent I've known has a few actors that they particularly love and believe in and want to help succeed. Call casting agents located in your city or in cities near your town and ask them who their favorite clients are.

- Attend theater productions at local playhouses as well as at nearby universities or community colleges. Start saving the playbills of productions you attend, circle the actors who were standouts, and keep them in a file folder titled "Actors." (Or take photos of the actors' headshots and bios in the playbills and email them to yourself, tagging the emails "Actors" or "Casting.")

- Watch the TikTok videos of people who live in or near your hometown. Notice if anyone seems particularly natural on camera, has special appeal or otherwise holds your attention.

Once you find people that interest you, search online to see if they have their own website or other social media presence. If they're an actor, see if they have sketch comedy videos or acting reels you can watch on YouTube.

Be Reasonably Certain Before You Approach Someone

It's of course wise to try to fully research actors before you approach them. You want to hear their speaking voice, see if they are particularly good with either comedic or dramatic material, and find out what their current physical appearance is. Looking at their posts on Instagram, TikTok, and Facebook will likely give you at least some idea of their personality and attitude, which might give you an idea about how pleasant (or unpleasant) it might be to work with them. If you decide you're really interested, you might want to contact them on their website first, rather than on social media.

Meanwhile, at every place you visit in person—restaurants, bars, grocery stores, veterinarian offices, etc.—keep your eyes open for anyone who has personality or is either attractive, quirky, warm, funny, or personable, or who is otherwise engaging or interesting to watch.

When I'm out and about and I meet someone interesting and want to ask them for their contact info (after I've observed them for a bit to see what their personality is like), I usually first ask if they're an actor. If they don't act but they seem open to the idea, I tell them I make small independent films. I then explain that when I see or meet someone interesting, I like to get their contact info in case I one day have a scene or role for them to consider.

Auditioning Actors

I now usually just meet actors in person, for coffee, to get a feel for what roles I could cast them in or create with them in mind. But when I made *What Other Couples Do*, I only knew who I wanted for three of the roles. My producing partners—Jimmy and our longtime close friend, Sherise Dorf—and I had to find six more actors for the ensemble cast. So Sherise and I set an old video camera I owned (the Panasonic DVX100!) on a tripod at her house and we had a steady stream of actors come in to read for the remaining roles. It was a blast! We found the actors on the Upright Citizens Brigade website, in yoga classes, etc., and some were generous enough to refer us to friends who were actors.

What to Pay the Cast

When you're ready to offer roles, ask the actors if the pay rate suggested by SAG's New Media or Micro-Budget Project guidelines is acceptable to them, or offer less or more, depending on what you can afford.

If you plan to work at a pace that allows a balanced life (shooting for a few hours here, a few hours there, rather than working 12-hour days for two weeks, for instance), paying actors a $100-200 day rate for a bunch of partial days will become expensive. Since a more easygoing shooting schedule is likely as convenient for your cast as it is for you (I've not yet met an actor who prioritizes an indie shoot over studio opportunities, and I understand the reasons why), you could offer to pay a specific day rate every time they log 10 hours.

If necessary, you could ask the actors if they're willing to consider working for deferred pay. But as I said earlier, some of my actor friends have told me they prefer to receive pay at the time services are rendered. Not just because they are working and want to be paid, but also because it confers respect. They're doing a job, not pursuing a hobby.

I think it's best to have a "most favored nation" approach (i.e., offer everyone the same pay for equal work). If you decide to pay some actors more than others for equal work, be prepared to explain or defend this choice.

Use a film production forms app (like Easy Release Pro) to collect signatures for release forms, or print boilerplate contracts from the net, write in the mutually agreed upon pay rate, and ask all the actors to sign one before production starts.

Offering Percentage Points

If you offer percentage points to your producing partner(s), DP, actors, or others, specify that they will begin receiving their share of profits from streaming platforms after you've recouped your production costs.

Consider capping the amount that profit participants receive or put a limit on the number of years they'll receive profits. If you don't, you will be responsible for painstakingly adding up long columns of pennies and fractions of pennies every quarter, year in and year out, until kingdom come. Also, you'll need to consider what will happen if you die before your profit participants do. Will a family member or third party take over the bookkeeping and continue to send out checks? If so, you need to cover this in your will. If you do not want to be responsible for this, then you need to stipulate to the profit participants that participation/your responsibility to them ends with your passing.

Chapter 4

The Script

The best insurance for making a good film is to start with a good script. If you're a little uncertain about your script, it can make a traditional, $35K-plus production experience even more stressful than normal. But with the "almost-no-budget" approach to filmmaking, some uncertainty is okay.

Here's why:

When you shoot solo, you're not under the gun to capture—no, *nail*—a story in just 12 days, say, like you are during a proper shoot. Instead, when you have the luxury of working one-on-one with actors over any amount of time you want, you can *discover* your story. You can see what direction you want to go based on footage you get of preliminary exploratory scenes that are either scripted, loosely outlined, or completely improvised.

In other words, *you can experiment. You can play.*

I think you can imagine how hard it is to experiment or play during a typical traditional shoot, when you're hemorrhaging money and there are 10-20 people waiting for you to get the shot and move on to the next setup.

But whether you write a script in advance or arrive at a story or outline through some preliminary exploration with actors, you're going to want to tailor the script or outline to an almost-no-budget shoot.

Thinking About Setting

For affordability and ease of planning, you can't beat shooting in just one (free) location. This constraint can actually be liberating—it forces you to focus on story, character development, and dialogue. And there are a lot of great one-location movies to inspire you. In addition to checking out the British film, *Abigail's Party*, by Mike Leigh, you might also want to watch *Tape*, written by Stephen Belber and directed by Richard Linklater. And *The Anniversary Party*, co-written and co-directed by Jennifer Jason Leigh and Alan Cumming. Or even the stage play that Robert Altman shot in the '70s, called *Come Back to the 5 & Dime, Jimmy Dean, Jimmy Dean*.

If you want to tell a story that takes place in multiple settings, it's of course possible to "steal" certain locations (i.e., work without shooting permits obtained from your city). I've shot with minimal gear—so as not to attract attention—in parks; on sidewalks; in front of houses, restaurants, and shops; and in offices, parking lots, and alleys.

For convenience and minimal stress though, my favorite shooting locations are my own home, my own backyard, my driveway and car, and in my actor friends' own apartments, houses, and cars.

Some think you should keep things simple and work with only two to four actors. I did not heed this advice in the making of *This Fucking Town*—it features a big cast. But your job as a producer might be easier if you have only a couple of actors to schedule with. Coordinating shoot times with actors is, to me, the most tedious task in low-budget filmmaking. Endless emailing back and forth as you try to pick a date and time that works for everyone is miserable. I've not yet tried any scheduling apps, but I've heard good things about using Doodle polls and am eager to try it.

Make a List of Free Resources

List everything you own or could get your hands on that could be useful in a film, including vehicles, locations, props, and wardrobe. For example, if your uncle bought a Corvette when he was having a midlife crisis and you think he might let you use it, put it on the list.

Props can be any items lying around your house, or that are otherwise easily attainable, that could be useful or interesting. For example, the Duplass brothers had a pair of upholstered chairs that were the inspiration for their feature, *The Puffy Chair*.

How to Decide What to Write

"Write what you know" is the advice you usually hear. I've seen so many people's writing dramatically improve once they started writing from their own lived experience. I think it's particularly ideal to write about an event or situation that you're currently experiencing or have just recently experienced.

If you "write from where you're standing," things will be fresh in your mind and you'll naturally include details that will bring the story to life. And the odds are good that you'll manage to capture something true and honest about the human condition. Those "real" bits will resonate with an audience, causing them to *feel* something, which, to me, is the main goal of filmmaking.

Here's how I decide what my next script will be about:

1. I write down what I've been experiencing or going through recently in my life.

2. I make a list of all the things I'm currently obsessed with—the things I talk and think about most often. Ideas or questions I've been debating in my head or with the people in my life, my favorite topics, and any interests, hobbies or passions.

3. I think of potential premises, plotlines, and characters that would allow me to explore or use what I listed in steps 1 and 2.

4. Then I think about the plotlines I've generated and decide which one I feel most compelled to write. Usually there's only one that I am really pulled toward, that I feel I *must* write.

If you write a script for a film that comes from the brainstorming process above, it's likely you'll make something original and interesting.

Sofia Coppola has said that her favorite films are ones that could only have been made by the person who made them. (For example, films like Bob Fosse's *All That Jazz*, Francois Truffaut's *The 400 Blows*, Wallace Shawn and Andre Gregory's *My Dinner with Andre*, and Albert Brooks' *Modern Romance*.)

What is the film that only you could make?

Chasing What the Market Wants

When I was writing spec scripts in my 20s and 30s, I could generate enthusiasm for almost any idea that I thought might sell. Now, I find it nearly impossible to make myself write anything I don't really, really want to write.

If you find yourself struggling while working on some script that you feel you "should" write, that you think might be "commercial," that you don't really love but you think would be "smart" to hammer out, ask yourself: Is it just garden variety resistance you're dealing with? Or is it actually your subconscious refusing to participate in a project you're not passionate about? If it's the latter, you should abandon the project and work on whatever lights you up.

If you're bound and determined to write and shoot something that you think will sell in a bidding war at one of the major film festivals, surely you don't need to be told that bidding wars—or sales in general—are extremely rare, and it's nearly impossible to predict what will be a winner. But here's a little story that I hope convinces you:

We once had a meeting with a respected producer who mentioned that he and his team had recently intentionally tried to craft a film that would get into Sundance. At the time, gender inequality in the entertainment industry was a hot topic and film festivals were more interested in choosing women-centered projects. The producer thought he was in good shape because he was working with a talented, popular woman writer-director who has huge followings on Twitter and Instagram (and she also happens to be beautiful, not that this should matter or even be mentioned here, there, or anywhere, ever, but we all know perception is often everything). Her script about a young woman coming of age was "edgy," the cast was full of stars, and the art direction, wardrobe, and music were cool. Even with all these boxes checked, the film did not get into Sundance.

Instead of writing what you think you should write, write the story you *have* to write, the story you are dying to make into a movie.

Screenwriting Basics

If you've never written a script, the key thing to know is that there must be a strong enough source of conflict to power your story all the way through to the climax. The most common problem with beginners' scripts is that they don't hold the reader's attention, either because not enough happens or because they haven't squeezed out all of the drama from the premise.

Your lead character must want something: to win the love of another person, overcome a problem, survive an ordeal, or attain a prized object or goal. And there must be obstacles to their getting it. Also, they must learn something about themselves during the struggle, such that they are a changed person by the end of the story.

Typically, a screenplay is composed of three acts:

In Act I (usually pages 1–25 in a feature-length script), the protagonist, supporting characters, and antagonist are introduced and the main conflict or story is set up, as well as any subplots.

In Act II (usually pages 25–75), complications keep developing as the hero experiences a series of alternating wins and setbacks on the way to their goal.

In Act III (usually pages 75–100), the action builds to a climax, which is either a showdown with their enemy or a final test from life/the powers that be, usually accompanied by an emotional breakdown and breakthrough. The conflict is resolved and sometimes there is a short amount of falling action.

Mystery writer Sue Grafton observed that writing is a profession that requires a long apprenticeship. It usually takes years to become good. Reading how-to books on screenwriting can help you learn and grow more quickly.

I think Blake Snyder's book, *Save the Cat!*, is by far the best. One of the first things he does in the book is ask you to determine which of 10 classic types of stories yours most resembles. (He gives many examples of popular films for each type.) He then takes you through a process of massaging your premise and the traits of your characters to maximize the potential for conflict.

He explains how good storytelling is not formulaic, but instead hits all the right notes. And he demonstrates how to hit all the right notes by walking you through his "BSBS"— Blake Snyder Beat Sheet. (Beats are "story beats," also known as plot points.)

His follow-up book, *Save the Cat! Goes to the Movies,* is equally fantastic. In it, he neatly lays out the story beats of 50 famous films. You learn so much by reading each of these beat sheets, one after the other, that I can't emphasize enough how helpful it is. You really start to get a hang of the rhythm and patterns of good films.

The icing on the cake is Snyder's writing voice. He's friendly and funny, making his books a joy to read. I think they're a generous gift to writers. (From the tributes students have written about him online, it sounds like he was a wonderful person. He passed away in 2009. Such a loss!)

I also love Viki King's classic, *How to Write a Movie in 21 Days.* She has a great method for completing a first draft, the book is full of wisdom and great insights, and her writing voice is warm and encouraging. You'll feel like you've got a friend holding your hand through the screen-writing process.

Last book recommendation: *The Art of Dramatic Writing* by Lajos Egri. This one is challenging. In it, Egri advises you to narrow in on a specific thesis statement that you will set out to prove with your story. I always think about this when I'm incubating an idea for a new script.

Analyze Your Favorite Movies

A great way to learn how to write screenplays is to break down your favorite movies. You can download, for free, the script of just about any movie you want to study at a number of sites, such as Drew's Script-o-Rama.

While reading the script of a movie you love, identify the "engine" that is powering the story and see if there's a pattern to the conflict that's created.

For example, in romantic comedies, you somehow have to keep the lovers apart, right? Well, when I was studying *Notting Hill*, I realized that Hugh Grant's problem is that he keeps getting mixed signals from Julia Roberts. The pattern goes like this: She does something that makes her seem interested in him, then she does something that makes her seem indifferent or disinterested. This happens over and over again! Watching the movie, we viewers are constantly guessing whether she's truly invested in their budding relationship or not. (Until finally she reveals all her cards, in the "I'm just a girl, standing in front of a boy" speech to Hugh, at his book shop. By this point, he has been burned enough times by her mixed signals that he doesn't immediately react to her declaration of love the way she'd hoped.)

The engine that powers my favorite movie, *Valley Girl*, is the tension between Julie and her friends. They're not supportive of her relationship with Randy, because he's different—he's not from the Valley. The discomfort Julie feels because of her friends' disapproval eventually reaches a critical mass, and she breaks up with Randy even though she loves him. Later, she has a heart-to-heart talk with her hippie father, who counsels her to be herself rather than conforming to what others want. This, followed by an uninspiring reunion with her ex-boyfriend Tommy, contrasted with Randy's bold romantic gestures to win her back, spell the end of Julie's dependence on her friends' approval (when, at the high school prom, she literally runs away with Randy).

When you love a film, try to figure out *how* the screenwriter created its magic. What exactly is causing you to love the interplay between the characters? Why is their predicament "juicy" or gratifying? Is it because of the characters' personality traits, or the actors' personality traits or performances, or is there a wish-fulfillment aspect to the story's circumstances?

Ron Friedman, social psychologist and author of *Decoding Greatness: How the Best in the World Reverse Engineer Success*, says many accomplished people have attained mastery by studying the best works in their field and working backward to figure out how they were created. Reverse engineer the storylines of your favorite scripts to understand how they were built and how the action escalates to a gratifying climax.

Learn from Bad Movies, Too

They say you can usually tell in the first 10 minutes whether a movie is going to be good or not. It's amazing how often this is true. When you watch a movie that has gotten off to a bad start, instead of doing what I do and saying, "This sucks!" over and over as it drags on, identify *why* you feel you're not in good hands.

Maybe the main character is off-putting. How so? Do they say or do things you don't relate to? Or is it that you don't like the actor? Why not, exactly?

Maybe the premise is faulty or there's a glaring plot hole that keeps you from being able to suspend disbelief in order to go on the journey. How could the writer have made the premise or plot more believable? What could they have done to make you ready and willing to go on the journey?

Or is the problem in the execution? What could the director have done differently (with the casting, the performances, the choice of tone, etc.) to make you enjoy the story more?

Great Characters and Memorable Dialogue

A great character often makes for a great movie. The 1995 indie film *The Brothers McMullen* has two great characters: Ed Burns' "Barry" and Michael McGlone's "Patrick." Barry is self-confident and cynical and Patrick is morally rigid and neurotic, and their opposing expectations and world-views provide a lot of the humor in the movie. While watching the trailer again recently after not having seen the film for a few years, I was struck by the fact that it's centered on a key scene: Barry peeling a banana while describing how women push men to shed their "all-important shield." It hit me that this is one way you could approach writing a script: Come up with a scene in which a character shares their interesting or comical view on a topic, then build a story around that, exploring how their view is either challenged or corroborated by events that happen to them or the people around them.

Probably all the most beloved movies have at least one or two passages of memorable dialogue like Barry's banana analogy. Most people love dialogue that gets at an important truth about life or expresses something honest or resonant about the human condition. It's particularly great when these bits sound natural, not like a "speech." Although, now that I think more about it, when dialogue is really good, it doesn't matter if it does seem like a speech. (I just thought of one of my favorite bits of movie dialogue that is literally a speech. Maybe that's the way to go sometimes— make your dialogue an actual speech. On YouTube, watch the "Ford v Ferrari Carroll Shelby speech," from the movie *Ford v Ferrari*, and see if you don't get chills.)

Be Comfortable with Discomfort

When I was working as a receptionist at an early job at Morgan Creek Productions on the Warner Bros. lot, development executive Larry Katz said something I often think about: "We go to the movies to see people make choices we wouldn't make." Bad choices, or courageous ones, can set into motion a chain of events we want to experience vicariously.

If you are a prudent, conscientious person (i.e., if you have a high EQ—emotional intelligence quotient), you probably avoid making bad choices or taking unwise risks in your personal life. If so, you might find it challenging to come up with scenes that are fraught with conflict, that "grab the viewer by the throat," as director Billy Wilder advised writers to do.

But there must be conflict in a story to keep us watching. We must feel the discomfort and tension caused by a story's conflict in order to want the hero to triumph. Why not embrace the fun of getting to write scripts in which your alter ego does all the crazy things that you wouldn't dare do in real life? On paper, you can indulge the impulses of your shadow self—those parts of yourself that you reject or repress. (The concept of the shadow self came from the work of Nietzsche and Freud, was further developed by Carl Jung, and has been written about in various screenwriting books as well as in the fantastic book, *The Tools*, by therapists Phil Stutz and Barry Michels.)

How Long Should a Script Be?

On average, one script page equals one minute of screen time. You'll want your finished film to be around 87-90 minutes. (Of course, if you feel you need two and a half hours to tell your story, that's your prerogative. Just be prepared to spend more time and money shooting it, of course.) You'd be surprised by how much gets cut in editing—the viewer "gets" things faster than you think they will, so you end up making lots of big and small trims. You don't want your movie to end up light, so aim to write and shoot at least 100-105 pages, knowing that some things will be cut in post.

Chapter 5

Get a Camera... and Fall in Love

When I first considered the idea of shooting projects myself, I thought about just renting a camera. But I quickly ruled that out. I knew there was no way I'd develop competency, much less mastery, if I didn't have access to a camera for more than just short rental periods. Which is why I want to urge you to buy a camera, too, rather than borrowing one from a friend or renting one. You don't have to spend a fortune. There are good cameras available at every price point.

If you search "best cameras for independent filmmaking" online, you'll find options for all budgets, from Panasonic, Canon, Blackmagic, Fuji, and other trusted brands. Before you buy, thoroughly research all the cameras in your price range to see what experts say about them. Be sure to reference charts that summarize the pros and cons of the top recommended models.

If you're having a hard time pulling the trigger on a camera, you could rent one from BorrowLenses.com for a few days, to try it before you buy it.

I have a Sony a7S II. It's several years old now, but I love it. It's a 4K full-frame mirrorless camera, it can handle low-light settings, and it has a film-like shooting mode of 24 frames per second. (This makes the footage look better—more cinematic—than the typical video frame rate of 30fps.)

If you're considering getting the newest version of my camera, the Sony a7 IV (which currently retails for $2,498 on BHPhotoVideo.com), you might want to go watch some videos from a talented wedding filmmaker in Texas named Matt Johnson. He offers great, fast-paced instructional videos on his YouTube channel, "Matt WhoisMatt Johnson." He's good at quickly explaining camera issues in a way that's easy to understand and he doesn't make you wait forever to hear his bottom-line advice or info. He seems to use Sony cameras most often and offers reviews, tutorials, and his preferred camera settings for recent models as well as older ones like mine.

If You Cannot Buy a Camera

Use an iPhone. If you don't own an iPhone, rent one. Before I bought my camera, I was aware that good movies have been made on iPhones (famously *Tangerine*, for example). Curious to experiment, I asked one of the actors who's in all my work, Gregory Hoyt, if he'd be game to let me shoot random "scenes" with him at his apartment, on my iPhone. Even though we didn't have a script or use any added lighting, it turned out great! Mostly because Greg is a fantastic conversationalist and a talented improviser. But it proved to me that I could actually shoot an engaging film on my phone if I had to. So, if you have no other option but to use a phone, you should go for it. Research whether there is any special gear you want to buy or apps you want to use. Search "iPhone filmmaking" for tips on getting a more cinematic look.

Get a Versatile Lens

Some cameras come with a lens, but many of the more sophisticated and expensive ones don't. My Sony a7S II did not come with a lens, and since I couldn't afford to get a variety of lenses, I had to choose one that was really versatile.

After reading up on it, I got the Sony FE 24-70mm f/2.8 GM zoom lens (a new one costs around $2,300; a used one costs around $1,700). It allows me to shoot from a distance but also in small, cramped spaces like bathrooms and cars. It's great, and it's still the only lens I've shot with for six years now. Next, I would love to get some prime lenses, because they offer a sharper image. I haven't decided yet between a 50mm, 80mm, and 135mm. Although a 135mm is not as practical for filmmaking, I like shooting portraits, and longer lenses like this are more flattering to people.

Following is a more in-depth discussion of lenses. If you're not ready to digest this information, come back to it later, after you've been shooting for a little while and are driven by curiosity to learn more about lens choice. You can skip ahead to page 95 "The Most Essential Gear."

Short Lenses vs. Long Lenses

The shorter the focal length of a lens (for example, 12mm), the wider the angle of view. In other words, the lens will allow you to see a lot more of the total scene that's in front of the camera, but the image of the scene will be smaller (everything will be relatively small in scale so it'll all fit into the frame). This is key if you are shooting in a small or cramped space, like a bathroom.

A wide-angle or short lens expands the amount of space between an object in the foreground and an object in the background. For example, an object in the background will appear smaller, fuzzier, and further away.

Wide-angle lenses also have greater depth of field (more of the scene will be in focus). If you want to have an easier time getting sharp focus on all the actors or important objects in a scene, you can use a shorter focal length (such as 35mm). (Alternatively, you could set the aperture to f/8 or f/10. "Stopping down" the aperture will let less light into the camera, though, so you will probably have to compensate by adding more light another way, such as by adding a physical light or by bumping up the ISO. I will discuss both aperture and ISO more in the coming pages.)

If you use a wide-angle or short lens to shoot a close-up of a person's face, it will look a little distorted, because items that are closer to the lens (such as a person's nose) will be enlarged (a.k.a. the "fisheye" effect).

The longer the focal length of a lens (say, 70mm), the narrower the angle of view—i.e., a smaller portion of the total scene will be captured, though the image will be larger (the subject of the shot will appear bigger). A long lens compresses the amount of space between objects occupying different planes of space within a setting, making them seem closer together than they really are. For example, an item or person in the background will appear a little larger and closer to an item or person in the foreground. (You can use this to your advantage in low-budget filmmaking: You can make a group of extras seem like a denser crowd by using a long lens to compress the space between the people.)

Because of their shallow depth of field, longer lenses can make it more challenging to get sharp focus on your subject. And they can be difficult to use for handheld shots because they magnify camera shake.

A long lens will not distort the face like a short lens will. Also, because a long lens has less depth of field, you can let objects in the foreground and/or background be slightly out of focus or blurry, allowing the main subject of the shot to be crisp and stand out.

The longer the lens, the heavier, bulkier, and more expensive it will be.

Your choice of lens affects how the viewer will feel about the characters in your story. I saw a demonstration online in which a person had been shot in medium close-up with three different lenses—16mm, 35mm, and 135mm. Each shot had a different look and feel. In the 16mm medium close-up, the person's head looked big and out of proportion to their body. They looked distorted and seemed uncomfortably close, as though I were viewing them through a peephole. In the 35mm shot, the subject seemed to be at a more normal, comfortable distance from me. The 135mm shot was the most pleasing. The subject looked the most attractive in this shot. None of their features were distorted.

In still photography, 135mm is considered a classic choice for shooting attractive portraits. But in filmmaking, a 135mm focal length is often not practical, as it will force you to place your camera too far away from the actor(s). Because a long lens captures a smaller slice of a scene, that small slice will appear bigger and closer in your viewfinder. The setting you're shooting in will not always allow this. For example, if you're shooting in a smallish room, you likely won't be able to get far enough away from the actors to allow use of a long lens.

But whenever possible, I usually try to use the maximum focal length on my zoom lens (70mm) to shoot actors' faces—because I like actors to look attractive. But you might like the aesthetic of actors' faces being a little distorted, or you may want to influence the viewer's perception of certain characters by using a wide-angle lens.

Zoom (a.k.a. Telephoto) Lenses vs. Prime Lenses

With a zoom lens, you may often not be aware of the focal length you're shooting in. Turning the focal ring until you like how close or far you are from the subject is not as ideal as making a deliberate choice regarding the exact distance you want the camera to be from the subject and choosing exactly the focal length you want. Where you place the camera, and the focal length you choose, will determine how close the subject will seem to the viewer and will affect how the viewer feels about the subject.

Many cinematographers say that using a zoom lens doesn't necessarily save time, because you can change lenses while a scene is being lit. But when you're shooting solo and you're using available light, or you're the one lighting the scenes, not having to change lenses *does* save time. When I first started shooting alone, the idea of changing lenses constantly while shooting was unthinkable to me. Now that I feel more comfortable shooting, I'd like to add a couple of prime lenses to my kit. Prime lenses are said to offer a sharper and more contrasty image. I love the sound of that. I'll probably get a 50mm lens first, as it seems like a useful one to have. But again, when you first start shooting solo, I think it's smart to start with a zoom lens. A 24mm–70mm offers the greatest flexibility and is the best lens to get first, in my opinion.

When you go to buy a lens, choose one that has a single f-stop, not a range (such as 2.8–5.6). The lower the f-stop, the better—this means the aperture is more wide open, giving you more control in low-light settings. For example, one of the widest apertures you can get is a 1.8 (say "one-eight," not "one-point-eight"), which lets in a lot of light. Long lenses don't offer this wide of an aperture, but some offer f/2.8, which is great. (More about f-stops and apertures later.)

If you're interested in a lens made by a different maker than your camera (whether because it offers a wide-open aperture or because the price is appealing), be sure it's compatible with your camera. You might need to purchase an adaptor. I've read that sometimes you can encounter little hiccups or quirks with adaptors, or there might even be significant limitations. Since I was a beginner when I bought my camera and lens, I didn't want to take the chance of dealing with extra headaches, so I bought a Sony zoom lens for my Sony camera.

The Most Essential Gear

After you get a camera and lens, here's what else you'll need:

- **Shooting "on sticks" (a tripod) gives footage a more cinematic look**. Owning a quality, sturdy tripod is a must. You'll want to choose one that can handle the weight of your camera and lens, plus a monitor or whatever else you might end up attaching to the camera. (I have a discontinued Manfrotto tripod that cost around $300 several years ago.) If you get a flimsy, lightweight tripod, not only will it be the bane of your existence, but your camera and lens will potentially be endangered. This is an important purchase. Be sure to pick a tripod that is substantial, well-made and well-recommended. You can find good quality used tripods on Ebay. (Note: Peak Design makes a tripod that's particularly great for travel—it's lightweight and when completely folded, it is a remarkably small size. You might want to watch the video about it on PD's website.)

- **Extra camera batteries (six, ideally).** The reason you need several batteries is because your camera might go through battery power quickly, and you don't want to get caught without charged backups. (Note: When you buy Sony camera batteries, they usually come with a free charger.)

- **A battery grip.** I was slow to purchase one, but my camera goes through battery power relatively quickly and I soon realized it's more of a necessity than a luxury.

- **At least two memory cards.** When you're in a pinch, you won't necessarily be able to find the type you need in local stores. Order a backup or two online and be sure to have an extra in your camera bag at all times.

- **A neutral density ("ND") filter** in the size that's right for your lens, for shooting in bright settings. It's like sunglasses for your camera and it helps you avoid getting blown out footage, which can't be fixed in post. (I have a Tiffen that cost about $100.)

- **A camera bag or case, ideally one that accommodates two lenses.** For a long time, I tried to use stylish tote bags instead of getting a proper camera bag. I don't recommend this route. I recently got a Sling camera bag from Peak Design and I love it. Everything Peak Design makes is very well-designed by engineers, many of whom are photographers themselves.

- Sooner or later, you'll want to see the footage you're getting on **a monitor that's bigger than your camera's screen**—so you can better tell whether you've got enough light on the actors' faces, if their hair is slightly mussed, etc. I recently got an Atomos Shinobi 7-inch monitor. Whatever you get, make sure you buy any needed accessories, such as a mount and cables for connecting the monitor to your camera.

Get to Know Your Camera

After I bought my camera, I paid $32 for a four-hour Gary Fong tutorial online that explains every button and menu option on the Sony a7S II. It took me several hours to make my way through the tutorial because I kept pausing it to find the buttons and menus on my camera as I followed along. I ended up learning that there are many menu options and features on my camera that only apply to still photography, not to the filmmaking shooting mode. At first, I wondered if it had been a waste of time to learn about all the still photography options when I can't use most of them (being in love with video, I was not interested in still photography at that time). But I decided it could only be helpful to know about everything on the camera, if for no other reason than at least I wouldn't feel intimidated by all the photography menu options like I might have if they had remained unfamiliar to me. What's great is that, after following along with Fong, I completely got over my fear of handling the camera! Learning about all that the camera could do made me feel like I had already made important progress. So I highly recommend watching a tutorial.

Always Be Improving

For the first couple of months after getting my camera, I was learning so much, every day. Each morning, I would leap out of bed, excited to shoot practice footage. I'll never forget how alive I felt during that time. This thing I had dreaded—learning how to operate a camera—was actually thrilling.

When you're learning about a topic or developing a new skill, you will be constantly surprised by the discoveries you make along the way. It's like the proverbial light bulb turning on, over and over. And the excitement you feel when you make progress is addictive.

But there were also times, early on, when I felt over-whelmed by how much I had to learn. On days when I didn't feel as hopeful or optimistic, I would sometimes just take a little baby step—by watching a video on YouTube, for instance, or casually taking a few practice shots of the tablescape in front of me while sitting on my couch. What I noticed was that I always learned something new. Some of your biggest "aha" moments will happen on days when you're feeling the least inspired and just shooting random things around your home.

After eagerly consuming so many instructional articles and videos, I've come to really appreciate all the people out there who generously share their knowledge with others. And I am of course still learning. Recently, I bought a comprehensive book on photography with lots of example photos demonstrating concepts. It's called *Digital Photography Complete Course: Learn Everything You Need to Know in 20 Weeks*. One way to go about learning how to use your camera is to put yourself through the book's course or a similar intensive program. If you don't like the idea of it taking 20 weeks, go faster! Derek Sivers has said, "The standard pace is for chumps." Why not "be a freak" (another Sivers-ism) and learn everything you can in 16 weeks? Or eight?

Throughout the next several chapters, I'm going to tell you, in my own non-academic terms, how I have come to view each of the most important camera concepts. But first, here's a short summary of how to learn about your camera and its settings:

- Look for a popular or well-reviewed online tutorial for your specific camera brand and model and watch it to learn about all your camera's menu options.

- Read online articles and watch YouTube videos that explain and demonstrate these concepts: ISO, aperture, shutter speed (choice of shutter speed is an important part of still photography, but when shooting video, you'll typically want it to stay fixed at 1/50 if you're using a film-like frame rate of 24fps or 1/60 if you're using a traditional video frame rate of 30fps), histogram, depth of field, "how to get custom white balance," "how to use zebra setting in photography," and "how to get sharp focus."

- Get in the habit of constantly practicing taking test footage and popping your camera's memory card into the card reader slot on your computer to study and learn from the results. (If you've got a newer model MacBook Pro or other computer that doesn't have a card reader slot, you'll have to get an external one that is compatible with the ports in your computer.)

- Practice making changes to the aperture and ISO to see how it affects your footage. Shoot indoors in different rooms of your house, shoot outdoors, and get footage of your pets and your friends and family, in all types of lighting.

- **Practice shooting as often as you can.** This is obvious. All the experts say it. And you know it's true: The more you shoot, the faster you'll attain competence and eventually mastery, especially if you engage in deliberate practice. Instead of shooting mindlessly, use focused concentration for short periods of time to make progress on specific goals. Just one short session of shooting per day or a few days a week will lead to big progress over time.

Essential Camera Concepts

I've mentioned many of these already, but here is a deeper dive into the most important camera concepts.

Aperture

Think of aperture as the eye of your camera. It can open wide, to let in a lot of light, or it can close almost completely, letting in very little light. Aperture is measured in f-stops. It's counter-intuitive, but the bigger the f-stop number, the smaller the opening. For example, an f-stop of 16 means the aperture is very small, or "stopped down," which means less light is hitting the lens. An f-stop of 1.4 means the aperture is wide open, which means more light is hitting the lens.

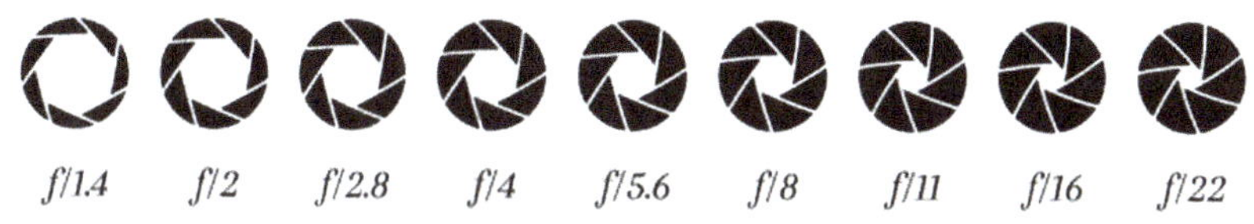

BRIGHTER TO DARKER F-STOPS

In addition to controlling the amount of light let in by your camera, the f-stop also determines depth of field. With a wide-open f-stop (f/1.4, f/2.8), there is very shallow depth of field. Shallow depth of field means there will be just a narrow plane of space in the setting in front of you in which the subject will be in focus. While your subject is in sharp focus, part of the foreground and/or background will be blurry, which gives you that nice artsy, cinematic look.

A higher f-stop (say, f/8 or f/10) means greater depth of field. In other words, more of the shot will be sharp or in focus (there will only be slight blur in the foreground and/or background). With a very high f-stop (say, f/22), everything in the shot will be in focus. If you're shooting a landscape, you might want everything to be in sharp focus. But in other types of shots, if everything is in sharp focus, your footage might look less cinematic. Having a little bit of blur in the foreground or background makes for more beautiful footage, usually.

Every lens has a different lowest f-stop. Lenses that offer a very low f-stop, like f/2.8, give you greater flexibility and control, enabling you to shoot in low-light settings (because a wide-open aperture of 2.8 lets in more light) and with shallow depth of field.

If you want to open up the aperture in order to have shallower depth of field and more artistic blur, know that you'll also be increasing the amount of light coming into the camera.

If you want to stop down the aperture so that more of your shot is in focus, know that you'll be decreasing the amount of light coming into the camera (and your image will be darker).

Shooting with a narrow depth of field makes it hard to keep your subject in focus. For example, if your subject moves forward or backward even just slightly, they will often go out of focus, so you will have to keep checking and adjusting to make sure you've got them in sharp focus. If there are multiple people in a shot, you usually can't keep everyone in sharp focus, unless they're all standing in a row or on exactly the same plane of space. If somebody steps forward or backward, they will be out of focus. If you want deep depth of field, where everyone or everything stays in sharp focus, then you should choose a smaller aperture (say, f/8 or f/10). Although this might make for a less artsy shot, it is a smart choice when you are in a high-stakes situation and absolutely, positively must get usable footage.

The reason you can't always shoot in the aperture you'd like to for either shallow or deep depth of field is because the aperture also controls how much light comes into the camera. You have to take into account the environment you're in. If you're shooting outdoors on a bright sunny day and you want to use a wide-open aperture like f/2.8 to get nice blur, you'll probably have to use a neutral density (ND) filter on your lens so your footage isn't blown out by sunlight. Remember, an ND filter is like sunglasses for your camera—it darkens what's coming into the camera. A good one costs about $100 and it's a necessity if you love shooting with wide-open apertures most of the time.

If you don't have an ND filter and you can't move to a shadier spot (under a tree or between buildings, for instance), then you'll likely have to stop down the aperture to reduce the amount of sunlight hitting the camera's sensor. If parts of your footage are so blown out by light that no information is recorded in certain spots, you won't be able to fix it in post.

Conversely, if you're shooting in a low-light setting, you might have to choose to shoot in a wider aperture so that you let in as much light as possible.

ISO

ISO (say "ice-oh," not "I.S.O.") determines your camera sensor's sensitivity to light. When you "bump up" the ISO, it's as if you are artificially adding light to your shot. It's a great option, because if you're shooting in a dark setting, you can add light without using physical lighting fixtures.

However, if you add too much ISO, it can affect your image quality. Specifically, it can make your footage "noisy"—there will be a graininess that's not desirable (the look makes me think of moving ants).

Newer cameras have better sensor technology, which means you can use higher ISO without it degrading your image as much. Search "maximum recommended ISO for (your camera model)" online to find out what ISO level on your camera starts to show noise or grain.

On the other hand, if you're shooting in low light, you don't want to tamp down the ISO too much because you'll be at risk of not getting highlights. (You can't add highlights later in post, whereas you can always darken shadows.) For example, if you're shooting outdoors at dusk and the light is fading fast, set the ISO high enough to make sure you can see the actors' eyes and read their expressions.

Another thing: If you're shooting outdoors at night, where the only light is from neon signs or street lights (i.e., there is no sunlight), and the ISO is low—like, 100—then you will mostly see blackness and the neon signage. As you raise the ISO bit by bit—without changing any other variables—you will see more detail, such as being able to make out a person's face and details in signage and buildings and other surrounding objects. Eventually, if you go high enough—to, say, 3200 ISO—the scene will be lit up enough such that it almost looks like daylight, which may not be at all what you want. So, be sure to stop at the ISO level that enables you to see just enough but not so much that the scene no longer looks like nighttime.

There's a YouTube video I found particularly helpful when I was learning how to get better-looking footage: "Photography Tutorial: ISO, Aperture, Shutter Speed," from Tek Syndicate creator Ward Hale (wardhale.com). I've included some of the best example shots from it below.

In a nighttime street setting, with neon signs and/or bright lights, if you want your actor to stand out against a pleasingly blurry background, try setting the ISO to 1000 and your aperture as wide open as possible (in this case, f/1.6), as in this shot below:

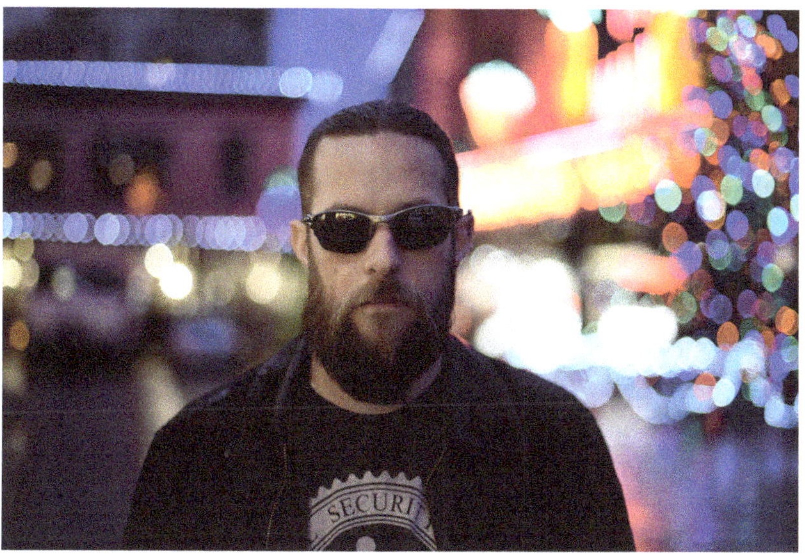

SHALLOW DEPTH OF FIELD NIGHTTIME SHOT

In the next shot, you'll see that if you keep the ISO at 1000 but use a stopped-down aperture of f/10, such that more of the shot is in focus, it's a lot less appealing. This shot reminds me of reality TV show footage:

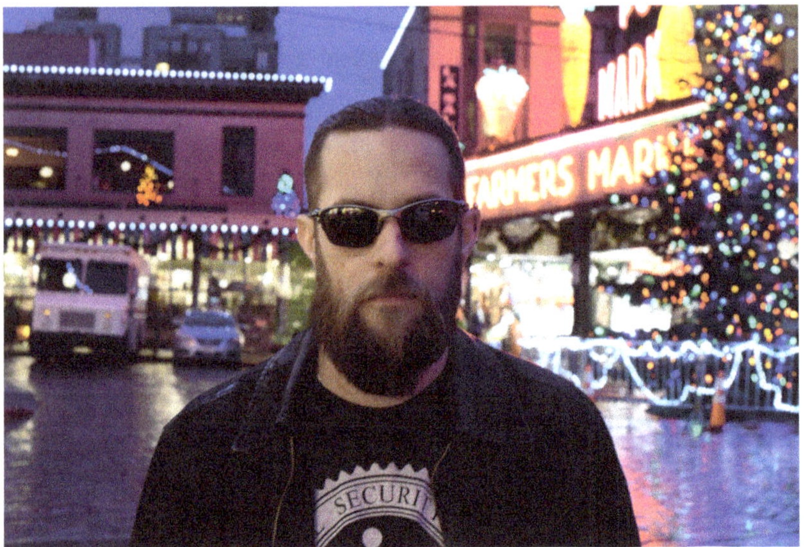

DEEP DEPTH OF FIELD NIGHTTIME SHOT

Similarly, everything is in focus in the shot of tomatoes, below, also from the Tek Syndicate video. The ISO is 640 and the f-stop is mid-range (f/6.3). There's nothing special about this image. It looks like a "big-chain grocery store ad," as the guys say in the video:

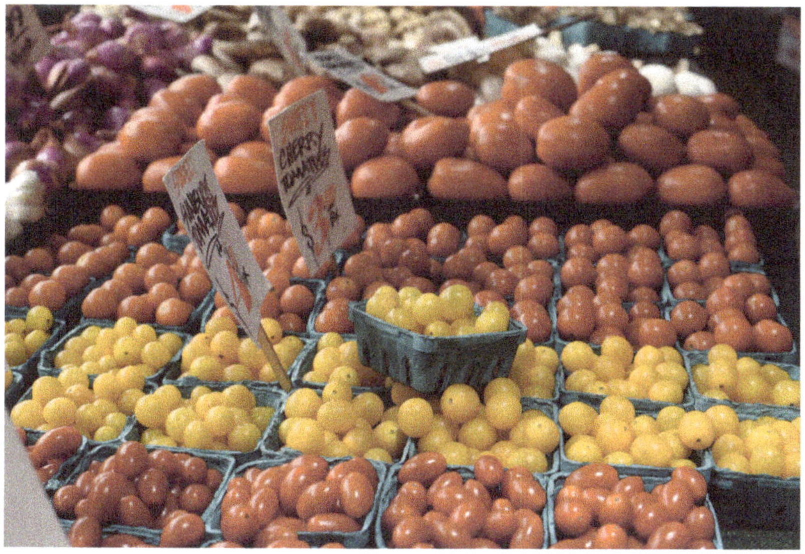

TOMATOES—DEEP DEPTH OF FIELD

But the next shot, below, with ISO 640 and f/1.6, looks a lot better. With the shallow depth of field, only the tomatoes in the middle of the shot are in focus. Everything else is blurry, giving the shot an artsier look:

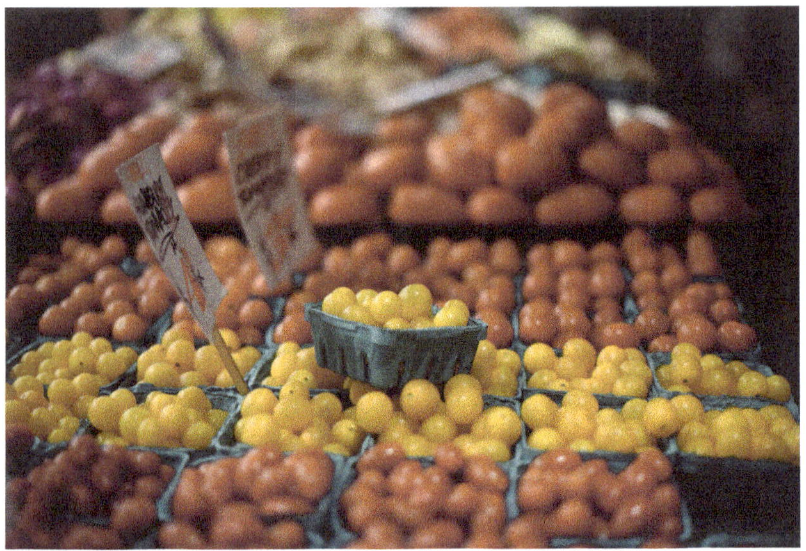

TOMATOES—SHALLOW DEPTH OF FIELD

Frame Rate

Film is a succession of still photos that move at a speed high enough to look like fluid motion. Each still image is called a frame. The frame rate of video is usually 30 frames per second. Some digital cameras offer a film-like shooting mode of 24 frames per second, which results in more beautiful footage.

Shutter Speed

Shutter speed is the speed at which a camera takes each individual photo. The ideal shutter speed is twice your frame rate. So, if you're shooting in film-like mode of 24 frames per second, you'd choose a shutter speed of 1/50. If you're shooting 30 frames per second (regular-looking video), you'd choose a shutter speed of 1/60.

Slow Motion

If you want to shoot action in slow motion, try a frame rate of 1/60 and a shutter speed of 1/120. Some cameras allow you to set the frame rate as high as 240 frames per second, but going this high can make the footage look "overcranked."

If, after shooting footage at a normal frame rate and shutter speed, you decide you want to make it look like slow motion, you can slow it down in post. But the result will not be as good as if you'd shot the footage in slow motion.

Important things to remember:

- Be sure to have more lighting gear on hand when shooting slow motion, because the faster shutter speed will result in a darker picture.

- Some LED lights have a flicker that is more noticeable when shooting in slow motion, so be sure to take test footage to see if you detect any flicker.

White Balance

White balance (WB) tells your camera how to read the color white correctly, without it having a tint that is too cool or too warm.

A lot of people don't take the time to get custom white balance for the setting they're shooting in, because if they're shooting in RAW mode (in which digital image files are minimally processed and uncompressed), the footage will contain so much information that it's usually easy enough to change the white balance in post using editing tools.

If you shoot in JPEG mode, however, your camera doesn't record as much color and tonal detail as it does in RAW, so you won't have as much information to work with when you go to correct the color in post. It's recommended that you either get custom white balance or use one of your camera's white balance presets, such as "Daytime," "Shade," "Fluorescent Lighting," etc., when you're shooting.

I shoot in RAW but I still like to get custom white balance each time I'm in a new setting or I change the lighting. Here's why: 1) Sometimes it's challenging to correct color in post, even with all the available editing tools, and 2) I want to get around the camera's tendency to average the lighting in a setting to produce an image that is 18% gray (or "middle gray"). (To learn more about this interesting and important topic, search "18% gray in photography" online.) By setting custom white balance, you're telling the camera how to see white as white (not as pale gray) and black as black (not as dark charcoal).

Some situations make it hard to get white balance. For example, restaurant interiors at night can have lighting that's so warm, your photos or footage will be yellow-tinted. If you set custom white balance, the camera will correct for the yellow tint, but you can then end up with images that are too cool/blue. I've found it is sometimes better to choose the "Auto WB" setting in my camera's white balance menu than go with custom white balance. If you have a moment to compare the resulting images from each choice before committing to a setting, do.

How to Set Custom White Balance

You'll need an 18% gray dome, which you can buy online from Gary Fong's website or from Amazon. Each time you change the lighting or move to a new location, you'll need to set white balance again. In order to do it more quickly, you might want to dedicate one of the customizable buttons on your camera to white balance. Here's how to do it:

1. With the actor standing in the scene, ask them to place the 18% gray plastic dome over their nose and mouth.

2. Go to the "Set custom white balance" menu option in your camera. (It might be at the very end of a white balance submenu, after "Auto WB" and pre-sets like "Daylight," "Shade," "Fluorescent," etc.)

3. Point your camera at the actor and zoom in to have the gray dome fill the circle at the center of your viewfinder. Press the rear wheel button. Select the color temperature shown.

4. Remember to remove your gray dome from the scene! I often forget to. See if you spot mine in a shot from *This Fucking Town*:

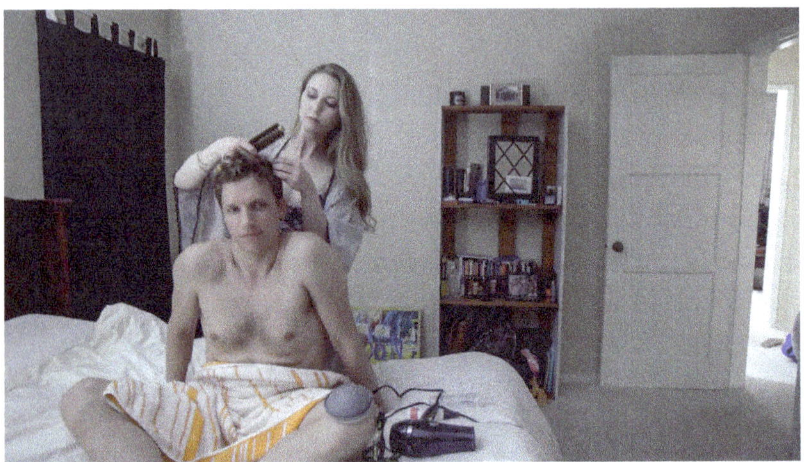

GRAY DOME LEFT IN SHOT

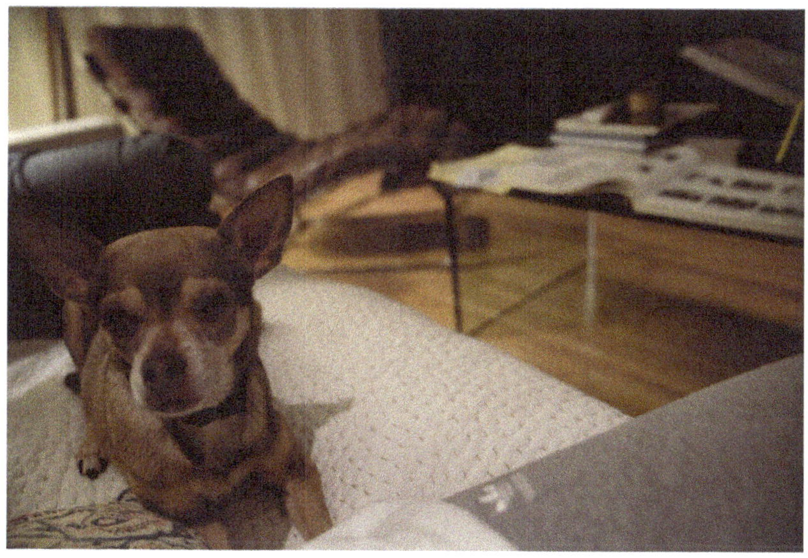

JACK—UNDEREXPOSED

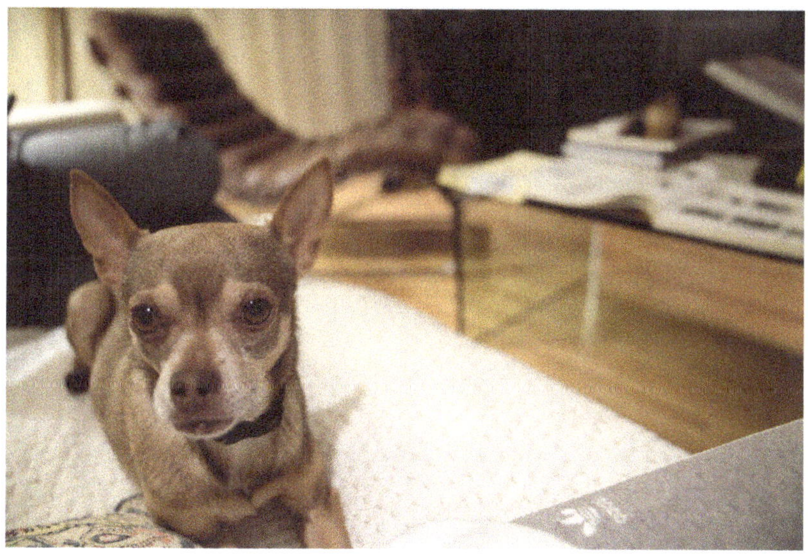

JACK—PROPERLY EXPOSED

The main thing you're doing when you're first learning how to use a camera is figuring out how to get good exposure (i.e., trying not to have underexposed or overexposed footage). When shooting still photographs, you'll spend a lot of your time "working the exposure triangle": experimenting with different combinations of aperture, ISO, and shutter speed to see how they change the look of your shot.

When shooting video footage, you'll likely only be changing the aperture and ISO, because typically you'll want your shutter speed to stay fixed at 1/50 or 1/60, depending on what frame rate you're shooting with (either 24 or 30fps, respectively).

Early on, I commented to my editor, Jason, that I just couldn't predict if my footage was going to turn out too dark, too light, or alright. And he said, "The histogram will tell you." As it happened, in my research online, I had just started to notice mentions of the histogram. Jason's confirmation of its importance led me to learn more about it. Turns out, the histogram is hugely helpful.

The Histogram

A histogram is a graph that tells you the brightness of your image by showing the tonal values—the highlights, the shadows, and midtones. In your camera's menu options, you can choose to have the histogram displayed in your viewfinder/monitor.

If your footage is squeezed to the left side of the histogram (below), it is underexposed (too dark). If there's even a portion of your footage climbing the far left wall of the graph, that means there will be a loss of information for the darkest area(s) of your shot, which you won't be able to fix in post.

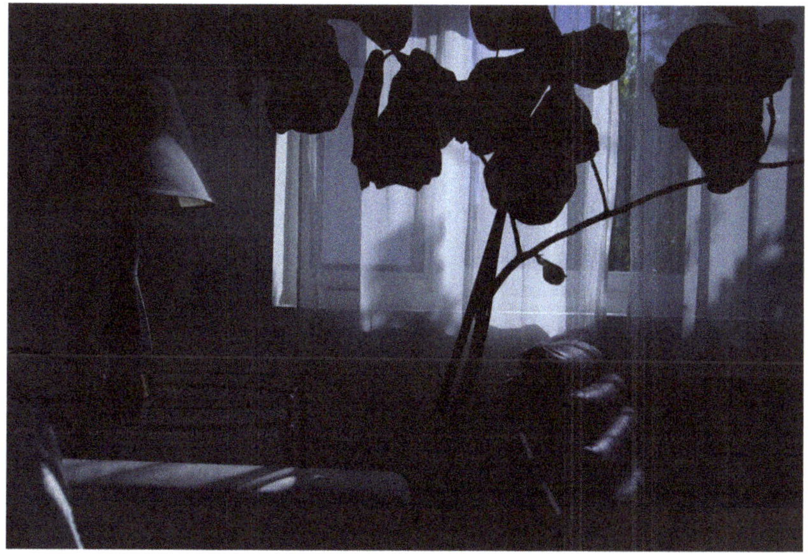

TOO DARK

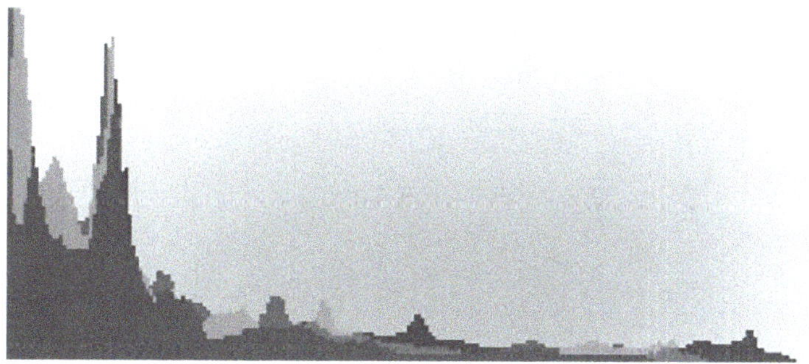

HISTOGRAM OF UNDEREXPOSED FOOTAGE

If your footage is squeezed to the right side of the histogram (below), it's overexposed (i.e., too bright and burnt out). If there's even a portion of your footage climbing the far right wall of the graph, that means there will be a loss of information for the brightest area(s) of your shot, which you won't be able to fix in post.

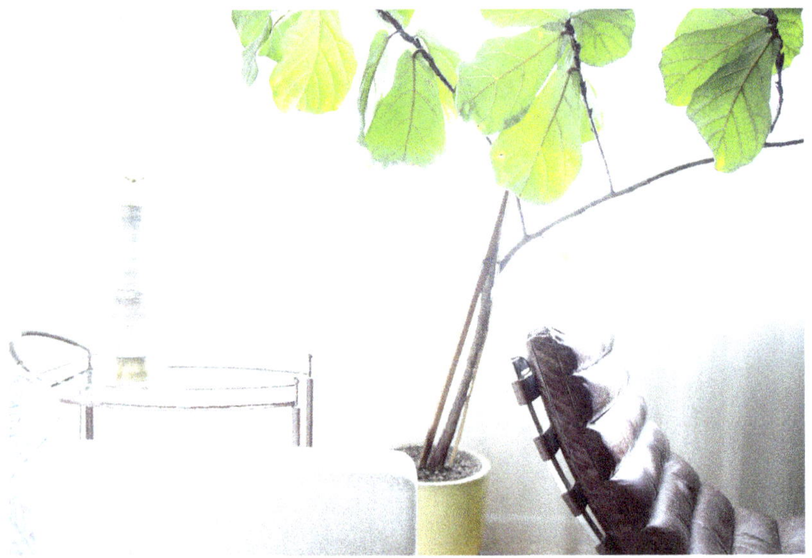

BURNED OUT

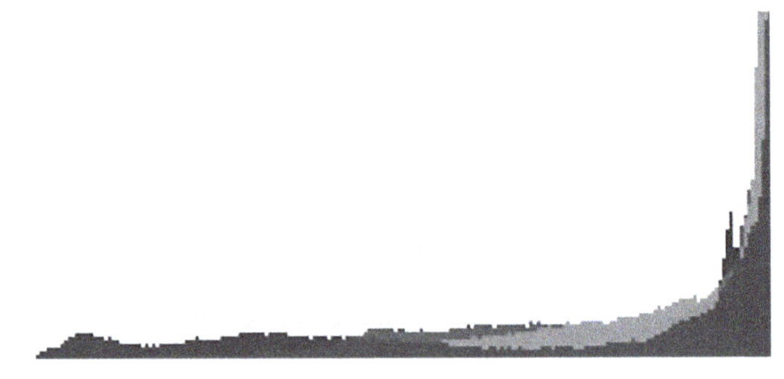

HISTOGRAM WITH BURNOUT

If the scene you're shooting has shadows, highlights, and a lot of midtones, your footage should resemble a mountain range that spans a decent portion of the graph, even if it skews slightly darker or lighter (to the left or right side of the graph, respectively), depending on the light.

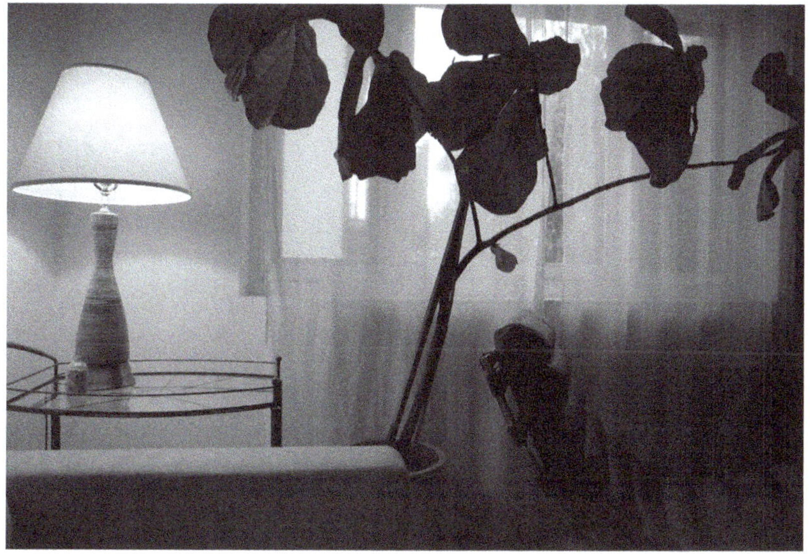

MORE MIDTONES

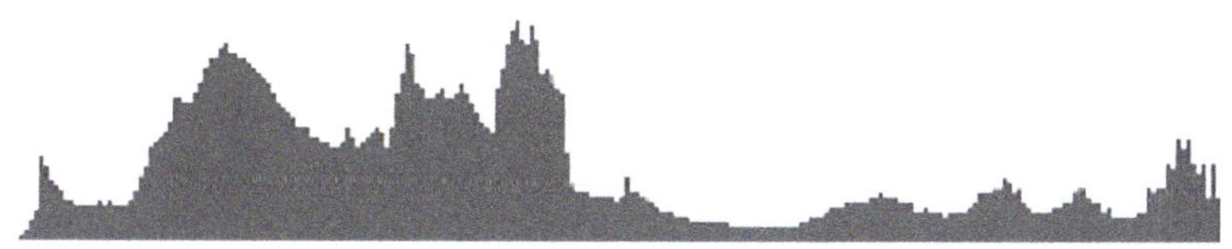

HISTOGRAM OF PERFECTLY EXPOSED FOOTAGE

If your footage is too dark or too bright, you probably need to increase or decrease the amount of light hitting your camera's sensor. You can do this by either changing the aperture or ISO, placing your camera wherever there's more natural light, or by using practicals (household lighting such as table lamps, floor lamps, sconces, etc.) or lighting tools (such as an LED panel, a softbox, etc.).

There are times when the histogram is not helpful. If you're shooting in a low-contrast setting, you might not be able to rely on it. For example, if your setting has mostly just light tones (like shades of white, pale yellow, etc.), such that it's light-colored or bright overall (such as snow in bright daylight). Or if it's composed mostly of dark tones, such that it is dark-colored or dark overall (such as a nighttime city skyline). Instead, you'll have to examine your footage in playback to see if there's information captured in the brightest or darkest parts of it. (Recall that blown out or "burned out" areas in which no information is captured cannot be fixed in post, whereas shadows can be made darker in post.)

Light Meters

A light meter is invaluable for getting good exposure of a scene. There are two kinds: a spot meter measures reflected light—the light coming from a subject or scene—and an incident meter measures the light falling on a subject or scene.

A lot of people think there's no need to use a handheld light meter anymore, since modern cameras have a built-in meter. But a camera's meter is reflective (it measures the light bouncing off a scene and hitting the camera lens), and reflected light measurements are often inaccurate. For example, if an actor's clothing is white (highly reflective) or black (light absorbing), it'll skew a reading. Still, there are times when a reflected light reading is useful (including, but not limited to, when you're shooting a landscape or wildlife—i.e., something at a distance, where it's inconvenient or impossible to use an incident light meter).

I have a Sekonic Studio Deluxe III L-398A analog light meter ($229). It came with accessories that enable me to get both incident and reflected light measurements and, per the instruction booklet, its "amorphous photosensor eliminates the need for batteries." There's something about the fact that it doesn't run on batteries that makes it even more fun to use. I love my Sekonic almost as much as I love my camera!

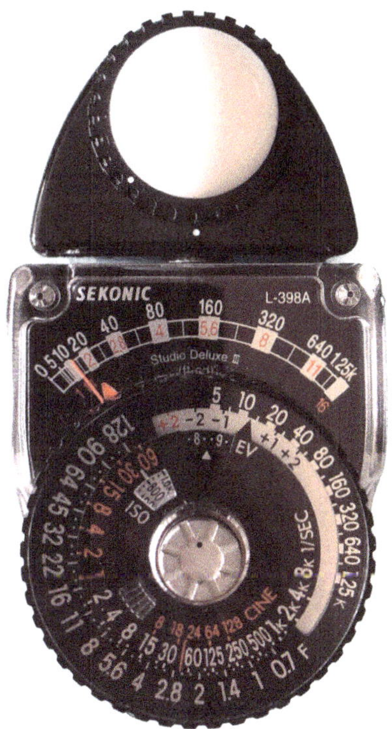

MY SEKONIC DELUXE III L-398A LIGHT METER

I'm going to tell you how to use the Sekonic, just to prove it's easy. (Exact use of other types of light meters, such as digital ones, will differ slightly, but the main idea will be the same: typically, you enter whatever ISO number you've set your camera to, then you take a reading with the light meter and it tells you what shutter speed and aperture combination to use for good exposure of your shot.)

1. First, make sure the black dot on the silver stopper button at the center of the light meter is at the top of the button (in the "12" position if the stopper button were a clock). If not, press the button with your thumb and twist it counterclockwise.

2. See the tiny window revealing the ISO scale just left of the center stopper button? Using your thumb, press the little ridged or textured area under the center stopper button to turn the small black dial that shifts the ISO scale. Select the ISO number you'll be shooting at (up to 12,000). (If you have some lighting tools, you'll probably be sticking to 200 ISO or whatever is the lowest possible setting on your camera, to avoid a grainy picture. If you are shooting with available light only, you might have to bump up the ISO to add light to the scene. Either way, you could end up experimenting with different ISO settings while preparing to shoot. If so, after getting an initial light meter reading at one ISO number, you can move the dial to a different ISO number and the recommended aperture and shutter speed combination, indicated along the bottom edge of the light meter, will automatically be altered. So cool!)

3. Hold the light meter beside or in front of your actor's face with the Lumisphere (the white dome at the top

of the meter) aimed at the camera. Press the silver stopper button at the center of the light meter and a red needle at the top of the meter will move as it measures the light (in foot-candles—the silver numbers that go from 0 to 1.25K). Just for example, let's say the red needle lands on 80 foot-candles. Let go of the stopper button. The needle will remain fixed at 80.

4. Under the main big black dial is a very thin clear dial. Turn that clear dial to line up its red pointer arrow with the red needle (at 80). (It's okay if the main big black dial turns along with the clear dial.)

5. Now turn only the main big black dial to get the black pointer arrow lined up with 80 on the foot-candle scale along the top of the big black dial. (There are two foot-candle scales: one along the top of the meter and another along the top of the main big black dial.)

6. Look at the number scales along the bottom of the light meter to see what combination of aperture (the number scale at the bottom of the meter) and shutter speed (just above the aperture scale) is recommended for correct exposure of your scene. For example, if you're shooting video at 1/50 shutter speed, you'll want to use whatever aperture is at the "Cine" (for cinematography) 24 mark, because 1/50 is the usual desired shutter speed for a frame rate of 24fps. (Look for the little orange line between 30 and 60—where 50 would be—on the shutter speed scale.) In our example, if the ISO had been set at 200 and the light measured 80 foot-candles, the nearest recommended aperture for 1/50 shutter speed would be f/2.8.

How will you know when you've mastered exposure? Photography expert Tedric Garrison said this in an article on PictureCorrect.com:

"The mark of excellence is in the highlights and shadows."

In other words, if the highlights in your footage appear pure white without being blown out, and if your shadows are black (as opposed to dark gray or dark brown) while still having visible detail in them (such as texture or pattern), you will have become good at getting perfect exposure.

Challenging but doable, right? But here's what complicates things: adding people to a shot.

Faces Need Light

When you shoot an actor in a setting, it's challenging to get good exposure of both the actor and the setting using only available light. For example, when you're shooting outdoors on a sunny day, you might stop down the aperture, so that the setting isn't overexposed, but sometimes you'll end up with not enough light on the actor's face. If you're shooting indoors on a sunny day, and you want to have enough light to expose your actor's face properly, it's hard not to end up with a shot in which windows are blown out. And if you're shooting at nighttime, you can bump up the ISO to get enough light on the actor's face, but now you've likely made the entire setting too bright—which kills the mood or ambience. In fact, if you set the ISO high enough, it won't even look like nighttime at all!

Your camera's built-in meter won't tell you if there's enough light on an actor's face—again, it just averages all the light in a scene to get 18% gray. You could set your zebra to 70 for lighter-colored skin tones or a little higher for darker skin tones, then experiment with changing your aperture or ISO until a zebra pattern appears on the actor's face (telling you they're correctly exposed). But again, your background will likely be too bright or even blown out.

So, here's one way to solve the issue:

1. Expose for the background (using the histogram to guide you, or a light meter). In other words, choose your aperture and ISO based on what will get you proper exposure of your background.

2. Then use *added* light (a lighting tool) on just your actor to get proper exposure of their face.

In the next chapter, we'll talk more about this.

Chapter 6

Lighting

Over time, while experimenting with lighting my dogs, objects, and people, I've had three epiphanies. And each time, I laughed, because I'm sure any experienced photographer or cinematographer could have told me these things right off the bat. But that didn't happen. Maybe these things are so obvious that many pros don't think to remark on them to beginners. What people do always say is, "Lighting is everything in photography," and the more you shoot, the more you realize this is true. But what they don't say is this:

 Just because you can see an actor easily, such as when you're shooting during daylight, it doesn't mean you don't need to use added light on their face. If you don't, they will likely look a little too dark or under-lit, even if only slightly so. Here's an example. The top image below is my brother-in-law, Mark Nadeski, with no added light. In the image below that, I used a short LED tube light (Quasar brand) attached to a C-stand gobo arm, positioned to the right of the camera.

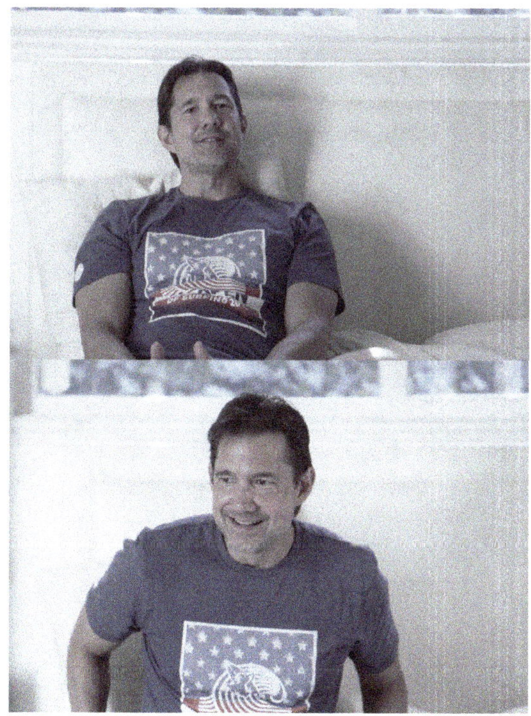

MARK WITH NO LIGHT VS. LIGHT

Epiphany #2: As I touched on in the last chapter, the trick is lighting only what you want to, and *not* lighting what you don't want to!

Epiphany #3: If you look at the room you're currently sitting in, you might think that if you took a photo or video of it, it would look just like it does now. But no, it won't! It will probably look flattened or compressed—which is why you want to add lighting. Because when light hits an area or areas of a space, it helps separate out the different areas of the space, creating more depth.

Following are shots of my husband, Jimmy, with no added light (top) vs. with an LED broad panel light (my LiteMat2 from LiteGear brand) positioned at a 45-degree angle to him, camera left, and an LED tube light (Quasar brand) at a 45-degree angle to him, camera right (bottom).

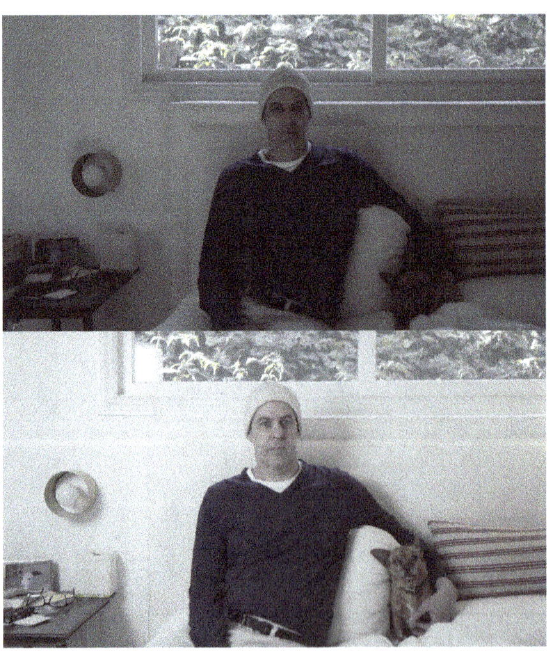

JIMMY WITH NO LIGHT VS. LIGHT

So, besides using natural available light (sun and moon) and practicals (household lighting fixtures like lamps, sconces, etc.), you might want to experiment with using added lighting to get good exposure of both your actors and your backgrounds.

Also, using at least one added light source is a way to make your footage look more cinematic. Because it creates shadows and therefore drama, it can add more depth to the space you're shooting in, making the setting look more like it does in real life.

Since *This Fucking Town* is more comedic than dramatic, I mostly wanted "high key" lighting (relatively bright)—i.e., I did not want shadows on the actors' faces or underexposed (dark) backgrounds, which are traits of "low key" lighting. To keep things simple, I used available light, practicals, and a broad lighting source (my dimmable LED LiteMat panel).

Any DP reading this will probably choke on their coffee, but a lot of the time I just aimed my LiteMat at the actor(s)/scene and often the only tweaking I did was turning its brightness and color temperature dials, to get either a cool daytime look (Kelvin) or a warm, nighttime look (Tungsten). I had a simple goal and that was to get enough light on the actors' faces to make them look good (according to my standards, not a cinematographer's).

As I've gotten more comfortable shooting solo, I've felt freed up to think more about lighting. Following, I'll touch on some of the things I'm currently learning about and experimenting with.

But a person can only juggle so much when they're shooting solo. And the purpose of this book is to persuade you to BEGIN. I don't want anything to stop you. So, if you can't do anything with the information below for a while— or ever—it's not a problem. Putting off shooting is!

3-Point Lighting

3-point lighting is a time-honored approach in which three different light sources are positioned around an actor to light them and differentiate them (make them pop slightly) from the background. Many modern DPs say they rarely use 3-point lighting. Instead, they might use just backlighting or available light along with some fill (in other words, they might only need one or two added lights to get a cinematic shot or none!). But it's good to learn 3-point lighting because each component serves an important purpose and there will be times when it's exactly what you want/need.

3-point lighting involves:

1. **A key light.** This is the strongest source of light (the main light) in a lighting setup. It can be a small, bright light or a broad, diffused light.

2. **A fill light.** This is a light source that is not as bright as the key light and is used opposite the key light. Fill light falls on the front of the actor and illuminates shadows (usually making the lighting on the actor more flattering). Fill can be provided by a light or a reflector or bounce board, to light the darker side of an actor's face to whatever degree is desired, and to make their face lit more evenly/fully.

3. **A backlight or hair light.** A backlight is a small light positioned at an angle behind the actor, illuminating their shoulders and the back of their head, to separate them from the background. A hair light is placed directly behind the actor and creates an

outline or edge of light on their hair and shoulders.
You can use either a backlight or hair light or both.

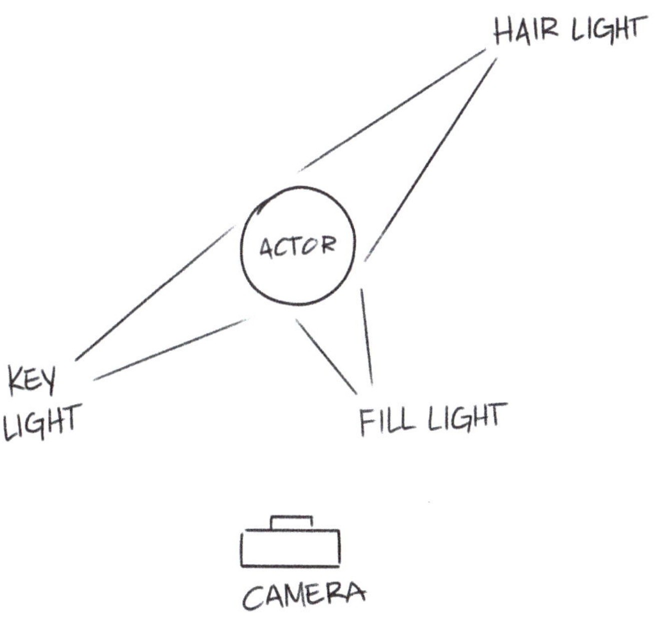

3-POINT LIGHTING SETUP

Following are the five most common lighting patterns
when placing a key light. The only one I have ever purpose-
fully set out to create is flat or beauty lighting, mentioned
first. If you start to feel overwhelmed while reading about
these patterns, consider this advice from Rickey Bird in his
awesome book, *Cheap Movie Tricks*: "All you need to do is
light one side of your actor." Kinda brilliant, right? And
doable!

BIRD'S EYE VIEW

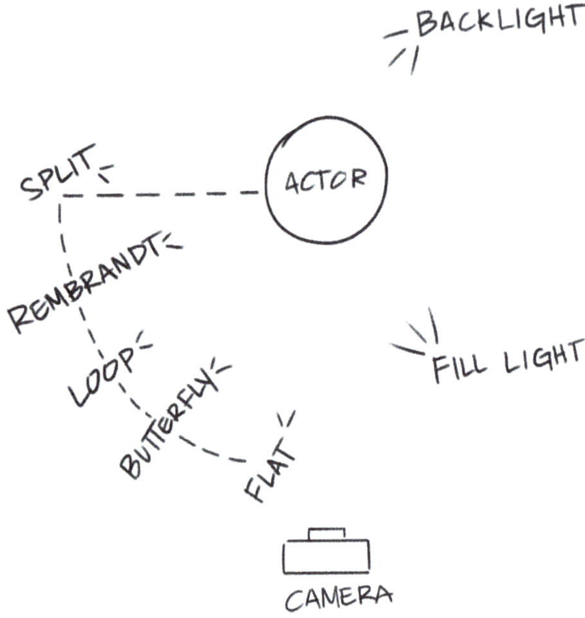

FIVE COMMON LIGHTING PATTERNS

1. **Flat** light—Used for beauty lighting. The light is placed just above the camera lens, hitting the subject flat in the face, filling in shadows under eyes and wrinkles. It's called "flat" lighting because it flattens the subject's features. There will be no definition of the actor's face and no drama.

The remaining patterns create more shadows, and thus, more drama. (If you want to practice creating them, it's easier to see the results on your model if you're working in a slightly dark setting rather than a brightly lit one.)

2. **Butterfly or Paramount** lighting (because Paramount film studio used this lighting for publicity photos of actors in the early days of filmmaking)—Place the

light above the camera lens at about a 25-degree angle from the actor (this creates a butterfly-shaped shadow under the actor's nose). A lot of the light will be hitting the actor's face, which will be flattering. You can also place a reflector below the actor to create "clamshell lighting."

3. **Loop** lighting—Place the light at a 50-degree angle to the actor, above the lens, casting a little more shadow over the actor's face. The shape of the shadow created by their nose will look sort of like a loop, thus the name.

4. **Rembrandt** lighting—Place the light almost to the side of the actor but not quite—it should still be in front of the actor's face (though not directly in front and not directly to their side). It'll cast even more shadow on half of the actor's face, but there will be a little triangle of light on the dark side of the actor's face (right below their eye, on their cheek). This lighting is more dramatic than the previous lighting styles, because there's more shadow. You can use diffusion to make it more flattering, but you would not use this lighting if you want to create a very flattering shot.

5. **Split** lighting—Place the light directly to the side of the actor, which will cause half their face to be completely in shadow (dark) and half of their face to be light.

You can also create a dramatically lit shot using **backlight** only. It's ideal if the actor isn't looking directly at the camera, so that you get a little edge of light along their cheek.

One Way to Approach Lighting a Scene

Always start with just one light. Set up that light, adjust your camera settings, then look at the lit subject to see what's needed next. Continue adding lights one at a time.

But before you do anything, see how the actor looks while standing or seated in the shot with only natural light. Observe the amount of light falling on them. Look at them through your camera viewfinder or on your monitor. Think about the story and the purpose of the scene.

I touched on this earlier, but when shooting comedic material, you might want "high key" lighting. This is relatively bright overall, with only a small difference (or "low contrast") between the lightest and darkest parts of the shot. For example, there might not be any shadows on the actor's face and the background may be bright as well (though ideally just slightly darker than the actor so that the two don't meld).

If you're shooting dramatic material, you might want "low key" lighting, in which there is a big difference (or "high contrast") between the brightest and darkest parts of the shot. For example, there might be one small lamp on a desk, illuminating part of the actor's face, and the rest of the shot might be underexposed to the point of being almost black.

Think about the motivation for the lighting you're about to create. Is the light supposed to mimic light coming from an overhead light fixture? A nearby lamp? A window? This can help you decide where to place your key.

To start, try placing the key light on the side of the camera that the actor is facing. This way you'll get a catchlight in the actor's eyes (a dot of light, which will make them look vital/alive) and you'll be shooting into the shadow side of their face (which is more cinematic). Position the key slightly higher than the actor and at a 45-degree angle to them.

Look in the viewfinder or at your monitor to see if the light on the actor's face is too bright. If so, dim the intensity of the light if possible, add diffusion to the light, or move it further away from the actor. Make sure there are no hot spots on the actor's forehead or head. If there are unwanted shadows visible behind the actor, place the light higher.

If you decide you want a more natural effect, try bouncing the key light off a reflective surface like a nearby white wall or ceiling. If you want to further soften the light, try placing a piece of diffusion between the bounced light and the actor.

If there are shadows on the actor's face that you'd like to soften or get rid of completely, add a fill light. Place the fill light—whether a small LED light, a China ball, a reflector circle, or a piece of white poster board—on the opposite side of the key light, at a 45-degree angle to the actor. If the fill is too bright, dim it if possible or move it further away from the actor.

To separate your actor from the background, add a backlight: Place a small light source behind the actor at a 45-degree angle, illuminating their shoulders and the back of their head.

For an added hair light, place a small light source directly behind the actor. If you find the resulting edge of light around their hair too noticeable or distracting, dim the light or move it further back, if possible. Often you'll get a natural hair light effect when you place an actor in front of or next to a window.

Sometimes Simplicity is Best

If you look for the video entitled "Roger Deakins on Learning to Light – Cinematography Techniques Ep. 1" on YouTube, you can see tons of amazing shots from movies the famed cinematographer has worked on. Toward the end of the video, Deakins talks about how a simple approach is sometimes best. He mentions that a lighting rig he'd created for the movie *The Hudsucker Proxy* was not working, so they "put up three China balls and were ready to shoot after lunch." Wow! And the shot (Paul Newman standing before a conference table of men) is of course beautiful.

In the video, Deakins said three other things that have stayed with me:

1. He gets bumped out of a scene if the lighting is not motivated.

2. While talking about the desire for simplicity, he referenced filmmaker James Wong Howe, who once said that early in his career he'd use, say, 100 lights to light a scene, then he got it down to around 10 lights, and he ultimately wished he could get down to using just one light.

3. He suggested that beginners should "go to Home Depot and get some bulbs," and "get some diffusion," and learn how to work with just these simple tools.

How to Get a Specific Lighting Look

Whether for creative expression or for visual consistency between shots, one way you can achieve specific lighting looks consistently is with contrast ratios (also called lighting ratios). Don't let the word "ratio" intimidate you— it just means the relationship between two quantities. A contrast ratio is simply a comparison of the lighting in two areas of a shot. For example, a comparison of your key light and fill light. Or your key light and backlight. Or your key light and your hair light.

A low contrast ratio means there isn't a big difference between the lighting of the two areas being compared. (Both areas are relatively bright or relatively dark, or they're both in the middle.) A high contrast ratio means there's a big difference between the lighting of the two areas being compared (one area is bright and one is dark).

Once you know the contrast ratios for a scene you're shooting (or a scene you admire from an existing film), it's like having a recipe that you (or a gaffer) can follow to get the same results, every time. Pretty cool, right?

To get a contrast ratio, you use a light meter to take readings of the two areas you're comparing.

For example, the next time you're shooting, hold your incident light meter beside or in front of the actor's face, with the Lumisphere aimed at the key light, and take a reading. Let's say the recommended aperture is f/2.8. You could then get a reading of your background light, and let's say the recommended aperture for it is also f/2.8. The contrast ratio is therefore 1:1—i.e., there is no contrast between those two areas of your shot, which means the lighting will be flat. If you decide you'd like for there to be a little contrast between the actor and the background, for a more interesting shot, you could reduce the amount of light hitting your background to create, say, a 2:1 contrast ratio. Which means there will be a 1-stop difference between your key light and background light. Your actor will pop from the background just a little and you will get a more cinematic shot.

For a demonstration of how to achieve different lighting ratios for low- to high-contrast shots, search "Understanding Contrast Ratios" on YouTube to find a great video from Dale Snood on the Vistek channel.

The False Color Scope is Your Friend

Another way to get specific lighting looks—and to confirm whether you're getting good exposure of skin tones—is to use the false color scope that's available on most monitors (such as an Atomos Ninja or Shinobi that you mount on your camera). There's something so satisfying about being able to see what's happening, exposure-wise, with each area of the scene you're shooting. The best part is you can tweak your lighting while glancing at the false color image, to see exactly how your tweaking is affecting the exposure you're getting!

You might find the false color image of a scene off-putting at first—it looks like a film negative, only it's full of crazy colors (colors that don't match the colors in your scene). These "false colors" represent different exposure values on an IRE scale of 1–100 (IRE stands for Institute of Radio Engineers; if you're curious to know more, search "explanation of IRE scale in false color scope" online). Some monitors show a key to the IRE scale next to or under the scope, which is really helpful. If your monitor doesn't show a key, you can search "false color scope key for (your brand monitor)" online, to see what tonal value each color on your scope represents. On my Atomos, red is the color used to represent the high end of the scale—it has an IRE value of 100 or over—and it tells you which areas of your shot are so brightly lit/overexposed that there will be no information recorded (i.e., you won't be able to fix these areas in post). Dark purple is the color used to represent the opposite end of the scale—zero, or below—and it tells you which areas of your shot are so dark/underexposed that no information will be recorded (i.e., you won't be able to fix these areas in post). Usually you want everything in your scene to fall between the extreme ends of the scale—somewhere between the yellow and blue values.

Here's an example of how to use the false color scope: After you've framed your shot and are starting to light your scene, look at the false color scope on your monitor. While keeping an eye on it, try tilting a desk lamp or other light source this way and that, casting light on your actor. As you change the light's position, you'll see the false colors on your actor's face change. You'll know whether the actor is well exposed, underexposed or overexposed depending on the false colors: If the actor's face is light gray—representing a value of 58–77 on the IRE scale—it's correctly exposed. If it's yellow (84–93 IRE), it's overexposed (which you might want if you're going for a hard-light look). And if it's red (over 100 on the IRE scale), it's burned out (i.e., you won't be able to fix it in post).

Another example: Let's say you don't want completely flat lighting of a scene because you're concerned about the actor and background appearing to meld together. Instead, you want the background to be slightly darker so that the actor pops against it. Keeping an eye on the false color scope, pull your actor away from the wall, reduce the amount of light hitting your background, or otherwise change the variables until you see the background become green or dark gray (which represents middle gray) on your monitor. Assuming your actor has stayed well exposed—i.e., a lot of their skin is light gray on the false color scope—you should end up with a pleasing contrast between them and the background. If, however, your lighting tweaks caused the background to become blue on the false color scope, you'll know the background is now underexposed (dark).

And if any portions of it are dark purple (-7 to 2 IRE), those areas will be completely black (there will be no details visible).

To learn more about how to light:

- Read *The Bare Bones Camera Course for Film and Video*, by Tom Schroeppel and Chuck DeLaney, a wonderful book covering the fundamentals of shooting, lighting, and editing, that is perfect for beginners but valuable for more advanced students as well. I can't recommend it enough.

- Research "filmmaking lighting" on YouTube. I found "Lighting 101: Direction of Light" from RocketJump Film School helpful. In the video, they demonstrate the most common lighting patterns described above (flat, butterfly/Paramount, loop, Rembrandt, and split lighting).

- Search "how to create 3-point lighting" on YouTube.

- Search "filmmaking using practicals" or "filmmaking with household lighting" and you'll find all kinds of helpful videos, including ones that tell you how to create good lighting using just one light. For advice on lighting a nighttime scene using inexpensive household lamps, watch "Filmmaking Tips: Using Practical Lighting" by PremiumBeat for Shutterstock on YouTube. If you decide you only want to shoot with available light, consider writing a story that takes place almost entirely outdoors. Watch Kelly Reichardt's movie, *Old Joy*, for inspiration.

- If you are not at all daunted by technical discussions of light temperature, etc. and would enjoy creating your own inexpensive lighting tools, read *A Shot in the Dark; A Creative DIY Guide to Digital Video Lighting on (Almost) No Budget* by Jay Holben.

- To learn how to determine contrast ratios for specific, repeatable lighting looks, watch "Understanding Contrast Ratios," from Dale Snood on the Vistek channel on YouTube.

- To learn more about using a false color scope to help you light a scene, watch "Cinematography Using Video Scopes / False Color, Waveform, Vectorscope" on the SonduckFilm channel. To learn more about how to get good skin tones as well as specific lighting looks, watch "Instantly improve your lighting with FALSE COLOR!" on The Film Look channel.

Recommended Lighting Sources

Once you have an idea of lighting techniques to try, you might want to buy up to three lights in your budget range and practice using them along with practicals and available light.

- Search "clamp work lights" on Home Depot's site. These lights are really cheap (around $10 each) but **they get really hot and can be dangerous. Wear work gloves when handling and don't let them come into contact with anything flammable.** As an alternative, you could try bulb lights that have a cage around them (also available from Home Depot). There are also a lot of work lights on sturdy-looking stands on Home Depot's website, for $100 or less.

- For diffusion (materials that soften light that passes through them), you could use a 21x24-inch Rosco white diffusion gel (about $8 from BHPhotoVideo.com). **If it touches a hot bulb, it'll melt.** So, when you attach it to a light with either black gaffer tape or wooden clothespins, leave room for air flow and curl the gel so that there's a gap between it and the bulb. You could also use a piece of bleached or unbleached (which gives a warmer look) muslin fabric. You'll need a frame to hold the muslin taut.

- A very affordable source of soft, diffused lighting that can be used as key or fill is a China ball (an inexpensive paper lantern with a bulb and electrical cord).

- There are also inexpensive softboxes on Amazon that come with their own stands.

- If you have a little more money, consider getting short Quasar Science LED tube lights (to use as a key, fill, or hair light).

- For broad, diffused area lighting consider dimmable LED panels that offer Kelvin and Tungsten settings. There are small, super affordable square panel options on Amazon and big, more powerful options such as a LiteMat, available in various sizes and forms, from LiteGear.

- Research "how to light with natural available light and practicals" on YouTube.

- If you can afford it, the ideal is to have three to four C-stands (to hold key, fill, and/or back lights as well as one to hold a boom mic pole). You might want one of them to be a Rocky Mountain leg C-stand (which allows you to shoot on uneven ground and stairs). You might need accessories to attach your lights to the C-stands (if you learn more about shaping light and want to try using flags). Wherever you purchase your C-stand(s), whether online or at a brick-and-mortar store, ask a knowledgeable staff member what accessories you'll need for the type of lighting you'll be using. Because C-stands are heavy and made of metal, it's important to learn how to use them safely and to wear work gloves while handling them. A quick, good video that covers the most important things about C-stand safety is RocketJump Film School's "Pro Tip: How to set up a C-stand" on YouTube. Another good video that covers C-stand safety, as well as sharing ingenious tips for getting the most out of them (such as how you can use the end of a gobo arm as a baby pin; how to mount a

key light, a fill light, and a flag on just one gobo arm;
how to lengthen a gobo arm; and more), from experienced (and amusing!) Dave Donaldson, is "Ep 33
C-Stands" on YouTube.

Chapter 7

Framing Shots and Getting Coverage

It's generally more comfortable visually for the viewer if you do not shoot an actor or subject positioned in the center of the frame (although Wes Anderson often frames shots like this—an example of someone making the exception to the rule their style). Instead, there's what's called "the rule of thirds," in which you position the subject or desired focal point in the upper third or the lower third of the frame, or the left third or right third of the frame, or even the upper or lower quarter of the frame.

Most cameras offer a rule-of-thirds grid pattern you can choose to have displayed on your viewfinder or monitor. (On my Sony a7S II, "Rule of 3rds" is one of the options under the "Grid Line" submenu.)

When thinking about where to place your camera for a shot of an actor, consider the most logical, sensible places first: 1) Directly in front of the actor, 2) at a 45-degree angle to the actor, 3) to the side of the actor (at a 90-degree angle), or 4) behind the actor.

Obviously, putting the camera somewhere other than wherever is logical or expected contributes to a director's unique style. Recently I rewatched Spike Lee's *Do the Right Thing*, DP-ed by Ernest Dickerson, and still can't get over all of the great shots in it. Another movie I love the camera work in is a '70s film called *Cold Turkey*, DP-ed by Charles F. Wheeler. And there's a small independent film from the '80s called *Morgan's Cake*, made by Rick Schmidt, that has also stayed with me because Schmidt framed his shots in a unique way and usually stayed in the same shot for the entire scene. He shot most of the movie "one to one" (or 1:1), he says in his book about the making of the movie, *The Miracle of Morgan's Cake* (which is well worth reading). Shooting one to one means getting only one take of a scene and shooting it from only one angle. (This is the way to go if you want to work fast and cheap!)

Zero tilt framing is when you set the camera to the same height as the horizon line. This is "neutral framing." From here, you can make a thoughtful decision about whether to aim down or up at your subject, if either (you may just want to keep it at zero tilt framing). If you tilt the camera up, toward an actor, it can have the effect of making a character seem powerful or even menacing. If you tilt the camera down on an actor, it can create the effect of their character seeming small, unempowered, or even poignant.

Getting Coverage

"Getting coverage" means shooting a scene from more than one angle. This allows you to create a "basic sequence" in editing, in which you cut from one type of shot to another (such as from a wide shot to a medium close-up). Shooting at least a couple of angles on a scene enables you to show the action from different vantage points and can draw the viewer in, making them feel like they're with the characters as an emotional event occurs.

Coverage might include any or all of the following shots of, for instance, a scene involving two actors talking:

1. A wide or establishing shot of the actors in the setting

2. A medium shot of both actors

3. A medium shot of each actor

4. A close-up of each actor

5. A shot from behind the actors

6. A "cutaway" of something else in the setting (such as a bystander, tree, animal, passing car, etc.)

"The most important thing to remember in shooting a basic sequence is that **each new shot should, if at all possible, involve a change in both image size and camera angle.** This not only makes the sequence more interesting" but it also "makes it much easier to cut back and forth between shots," says Tom Schroeppel in the fantastic book I recommended earlier, *The Bare Bones Camera Course for Film and Video*.

He explains that a change in image size and camera angle will often cover mismatches in the position of an actor's head, for example, from one shot to another. It's almost like, when you change to a different angle that features a different image size, you're picking up with the character just a fraction of a second later, so your brain accepts that they moved slightly during that time.

Storyboarding

Having a lot of coverage gives you options in editing, but too many options can be overwhelming and unhelpful. Also, it's time-consuming to shoot coverage. If you shoot most of your scenes from several different angles, you and your cast will likely find the repetition tedious. Instead, the ideal is to go into a shoot knowing how you want the finished movie to play out visually, so that you know exactly what shots you need. For this reason, it's smart to storyboard your script. Storyboarding forces you to think cinematically—to make decisions on what your shots, and therefore scenes, will look like so that you know what you want and need before you shoot. Although it helps to have drawing skills, it's not mandatory for storyboarding—the only thing that matters is whether you can understand your own sketches (making notes beneath your sketches will help). At the very least, before shooting, you might want to go through your script and think about which scenes you'll want more coverage of than others. It might be that you want the most coverage for particularly important scenes (such as emotionally climactic scenes) or frenetic action scenes.

Eyelines, or How Not to "Cross the Line"

If you're watching a movie or show and an actor looks in a different direction than you expect, such that you're confused about where they're standing or sitting within a setting, then it's likely the director or DP "crossed the line." You'll know when it happens because it's jarring.

How to avoid crossing the line: If two people are in a shot, imagine them connected by a string or line. You must place the camera on only one side of the string/line. You can move the camera for different shots, but it must stay on the one side of the string/line. With the person who is looking left to talk to their scene partner, they must be looking left in every shot you get of them. Likewise, their scene partner must always be looking right in every shot (whether wide or close-up or medium close-up).

If two people are sitting at a table, stay on just one side of an imaginary line drawn between them. If 3 people are seated at a table, imagine a line drawn between each set of actors and keep the camera on just one side of each set of lines—i.e., on the same side of the lines—for all coverage.

Dolly Shots

If you don't have the money to rent a dolly and tracks, try setting your camera on a smooth-moving item and push it to get the shot. For example, a shopping cart, a car, an office chair, a skateboard, or even a stack of heavy books.

Handheld Shots

The shakiness of a handheld camera will be less noticeable if the person or object you're shooting is in motion (for example, a person walking toward you) rather than stationary. Also, if you use a wide lens, the footage will be less shaky than if you use a long lens.

Handheld tracking shots are bumpier with newer, smaller cameras that are lightweight. To address this, you can attach the camera to a tripod that's been folded up and is carried (with the camera mounted to it), to add heft to the camera and thereby make it easier to hold steady.

How to Get Focus

Find "Peaking" in your camera menu and turn it on. After you've framed a shot, aim your camera at the subject and turn the focus ring on your lens until you see the subject's eyes light up with whatever color of peaking you chose (on my Sony camera, I can choose white, yellow, or red). If there's no one in the shot, fine-tune your focus until the maximum amount of peaking color is showing in your viewfinder or your monitor. (If there's only a small amount of the peaking color, your shot will not be in sharp focus.) Another way to get focus is to zoom in, get sharp focus on the actor's eyes, then zoom out. The shot will stay in focus unless you move the camera.

"Pulling focus" is when the focus is changed (adjusted manually) within a shot, generally to keep a moving subject sharp. For example, when shooting an actor walking toward or away from the camera. "Rack focus" is used to describe a shift in focus from one object/person to another within a shot. To change focus during a shot, you can put little pieces of tape on the focus dial to mark the beginning and end focus settings. For example, use a tape mark for focus on a subject in the foreground and another piece of tape marking the focus for a subject in the background. A good way to practice pulling focus is to put your camera on its longest lens setting and practice focusing on cars as they go past you.

When first learning how to use your camera, if you are shooting something more important than practice footage and are concerned about your ability to get sharp focus, use a smaller aperture (say, f/8) to make it easier.

Aspect Ratio

Aspect ratio is an expression of your picture's dimensions. The first number has to do with the width of the picture, the second number has to do with the height. The aspect ratios I like best are 2.39:1 and 1.85:1 because I associate them with classic films, whereas 16:9 is the aspect ratio of modern televisions (televisions used to be more square, with a 4:3 aspect ratio).

It's best to decide what aspect ratio to set your camera to before you begin shooting a project, because obviously it'll affect how you frame shots (and, aside from aesthetic concerns, you'll want to be sure you're leaving enough head room and capturing everything you want to within the frame).

Chapter 8

Getting Good Sound

As I mentioned earlier in this book, sound quality matters more than picture quality. If the sound in a show is bad, most people will become frustrated and stop watching, whereas if the sound is pristine and the picture is bad, people don't mind as much. (There are some persuasive videos that demonstrate this on YouTube. For example, search for "audio is more important than video" on Vic Barry's channel.)

Recording Sound with a Boom Mic

When I first began shooting by myself, I had so much on my plate learning how to use the camera that I felt like I couldn't handle trying to get boom mic sound. So I used only lavalier (or "lav") mics to record sound. But when I started recording boom sound (i.e., using a shotgun mic attached to a boom pole), the sound was so much better I was kicking myself for not tackling it sooner. A boom mic captures more of the ambient noise in a setting and therefore is much richer. It's the gold standard. I hope you'll get boom mic sound for all your productions from the get-go. Don't wait like I did.

To record boom sound while shooting alone with actors, I put my Auray boom pole holder in a gobo head on a C-stand. I then put the boom pole (with shotgun mic attached) in the cradle and position the mic just out of frame, to record dialogue while I'm operating the camera. Specifically, I position the mic just above the top of the frame and aimed at a diagonal to the middle of the actor's chin. Ideally, the mic will be just 1-2 feet away from the actor. I leave it in position the entire shot.

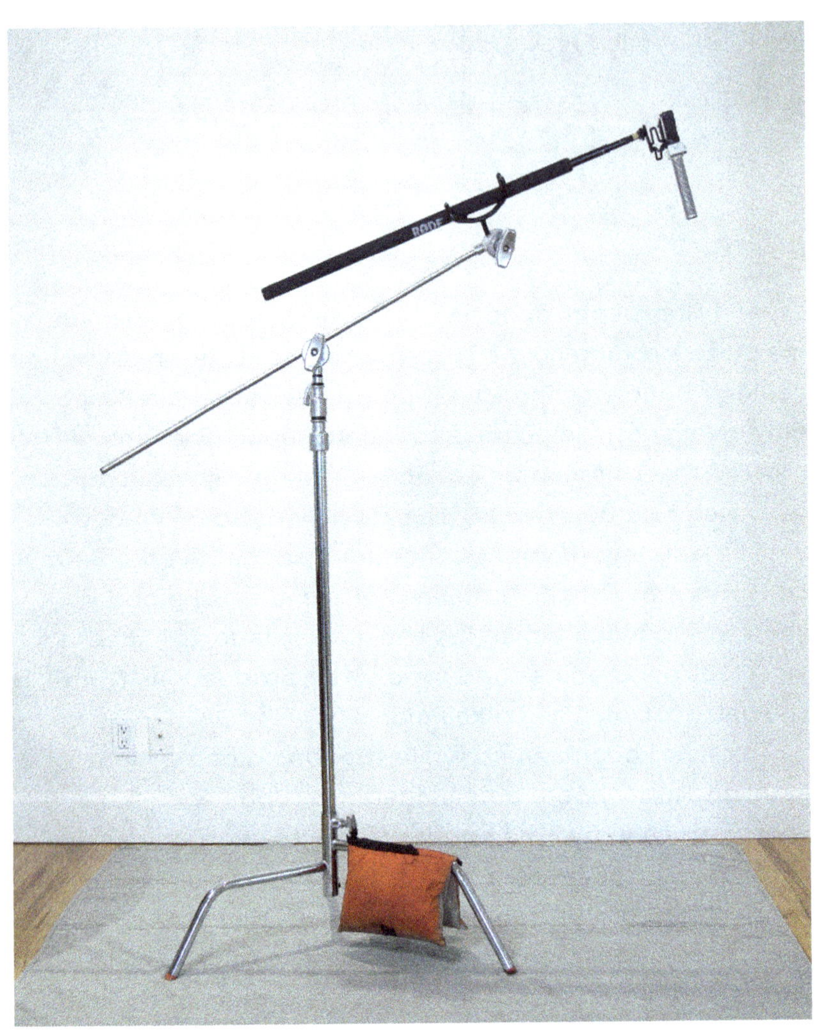

BOOM POLE SETUP

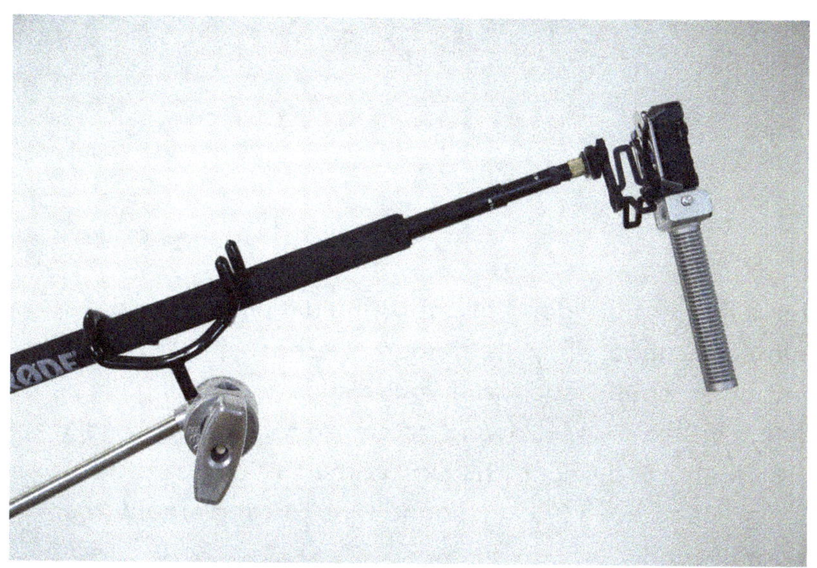

CLOSE-UP OF BOOM POLE AND RECORDER

I have not yet tried recording boom sound for an actor in motion, but when I do, I'll likely use a stopped-down aperture that allows deep depth of field (so the actor(s) stays in focus), I'll hit "Record" on both my camera and my Zoom F1 field recorder, then I'll hold the boom pole and follow the actor(s) as they move (leaving the camera recording, unmanned, while I record sound). Not ideal, but until I break down and get an assistant, that's what I'll be trying.

Recording Sound with Lav Mics

Lavalier mics are good at capturing dialogue but not ambient sound. They are a good alternative if you can't get boom sound, such as if you're shooting in a public place and want to avoid drawing attention to yourself. Also, if you don't mind taking the extra time to "lav up" the actors, it's great to have backup sound files to supplement your boom sound.

When you're shooting and moving fast, you'll be tempted to use the tiny butterfly clips that come with the lav mics, but don't!—unless you're doing an interview-style shoot in which it's okay for the mic to be in plain sight, attached to the lapel of the actor's shirt or jacket. I have found that when the lav mics are clipped to a layer of clothing (say, to an actress's bra), if clothing rustles against the mic, there will usually be unpleasant crackling in your dialogue tracks, which can't always be fixed.

I've also sometimes heard a weird vibrating noise under actors' dialogue, which might have been caused by the little spring-release on the butterfly clip being jostled. Just remove the butterfly clips from the mics and store them in the bags that come with the mics.

Instead of using the clips, use Rycote Stickies: Peel off two stickies and sandwich a lav mic between them. Ask the actor to attach one of the sticky sides of the mic sandwich to their skin, ideally between the pecs or breasts, about six inches beneath their mouth. The mic's wire must be hidden under the actor's clothes and the recorder must be stored in one of their clothing pockets.

Be sure that the cord and recorder are not visible when you are framing the shot.

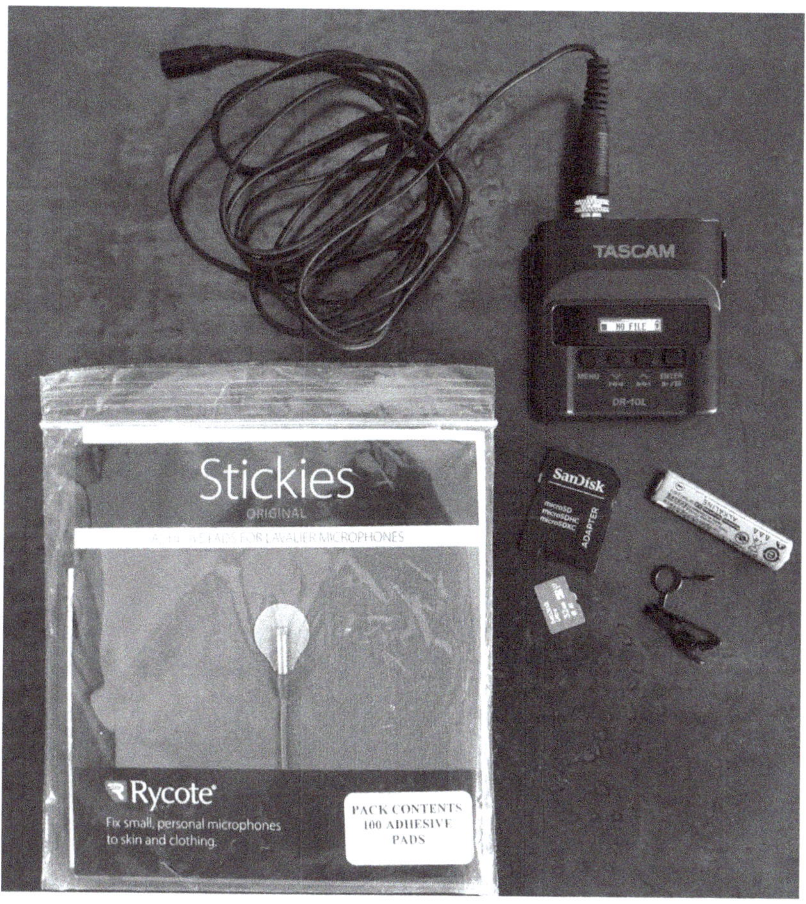

LAV MIC KIT

DON'T SKIP THIS STEP: Once the lav mic is on the actor, hit the "Record" button on the recorder, and ask the actor to say some dialogue. Then plug your headphones into the headphone connection on the recorder and listen to the recording to see if there's any crackling or other noise.

You'll be tempted to skip this step. Don't!

Tips for Recording Good Sound

Be sure to set the gain level on your field recorder each time you record. Gain refers to the strength of the sound signal being recorded. It's similar to volume. To set the gain level, record the actor speaking while you watch the needle or bars on the recorder's display to see what decibel level is being reached. -12 dB is the desired level. Turn the gain dial (usually numbered 1-10) up or down until the actor's voice (or other sound being recorded) hits a high of -12 decibels.

And be sure to record at least one minute of room tone immediately prior to or following every scene you shoot. (Everyone on set must stand or sit still and be completely silent while this occurs.) Room tone is the ambient sound of the room or setting in which you're shooting (even if the room or setting is or seems completely quiet, room tone includes the "white noise" hum of building utilities like heating and air conditioning, outdoor sounds such as birds chirping, traffic passing on the street, etc.). In editing, you'll put room tone under transitions between takes to make the changes in sound more seamless.

What else? Okay, two more things: Your in-camera microphone will capture sound as well. Even though the quality won't be great, it'll be useful later, in editing, when you sync the in-camera sound with the boom mic sound. Also, sometimes having in-camera sound recording will save your a—! Before I started getting boom sound, I once forgot to bring my lav mics to a shoot with actors Greg Hoyt and Annie Cavalero for a scene in *This Fucking Town*. Going home to grab the lav mics was not an option, so we had to shoot the scene with in-camera sound. But I was grateful to have that, because their performances were awesome and the sound quality was good enough!

Remember to use your slate, if you own one, or clap loudly in front of the camera each time you start recording a new take. Having a loud clap on your in-camera sound recording and your boom or lav mic sound recording will enable you to sync the two effortlessly later in editing. (If there's no spike provided by a clap or other distinctive noise, you will likely have to painstakingly sync the sound with the video yourself rather than being able to have Adobe Premiere Pro or other editing software do it for you.)

I've said it before, but I'll say it again: With sound, an ounce of prevention is worth a pound of cure. It is WAY better to make every effort to get good sound during the shoot rather than count on fixing it in post. Often, bad sound can be made better, but it can't always be made *good*. So, do record some test sound with your actor(s) and listen to it to make sure there are no clothing rustling issues, etc., before shooting your first take.

If You Want to Leave It to a Pro

Hiring a "sound person" (a professional sound recordist) costs $400 or more per day. The good news is that they bring all their own gear, and assuming they're good at their job, it's a luxury and a relief to turn the sound recording work over to them.

Most sound recordists are frequently replacing their gear with newer stuff. Also, they are typically freelancers and must pay for their own health insurance. When you think about these things, and when you consider how long and stressful most shoots are, their day rate no longer seems expensive. I love having a sound recordist.

The reason I often do without a sound recordist though, besides the expense, is because, to me, one of the biggest benefits of shooting solo is being able to keep a civilized shooting schedule. I prefer not to work a 12-hour day and instead have balance in my life. If you hire a sound person, you're going to want to work a full day to get the most for your money. Most sound recordists will not accept a portion of their usual rate to work a partial day. Understandably, most want to maximize their time, working a full day for their full rate.

An alternative is to pay a friend a mutually agreed upon hourly rate to hold a boom mic and record sound into a field recorder. Unless your friend happens to own the gear, you'll have to buy, rent, or borrow it. Keep in mind that it will be cheaper in the long run to own gear versus renting it, especially if you intend to make multiple projects. If you go this route, be sure to read the sound-recording-related advice in Chapter 1: The "Cheap Expensive" Route.

Recommended Sound Gear

Following is a list of the sound gear I have, but you should certainly do your own research before purchasing anything to make sure there aren't newer, better products on the market.

- Zoom F1-SP 2-Track Portable Field Recorder with Shotgun Microphone (~$229)

- Zoom SMF-1 Shockmount

- ¼-inch Manfrotto metal thread to attach the field recorder to the boom pole

- Auray boom pole holder

- Rode 3-section telescopic boom pole

- A C-stand with a gobo arm, to hold the Auray or other brand boom pole holder

- An artificial fur and/or foam windshield in a size appropriate for your shotgun mic (to reduce wind noise when shooting outdoors)

- Two Tascam DR-10L audio recorders with lav mics

- Rycote Stickies (package of 100; you'll go through them faster than you think). If you don't need the hypoallergenic kind, don't get them. Get the regular ones, which adhere to skin better.

- A Rode VideoMic Pro Camera-mount Shotgun Microphone to slide into the shoe mount on your camera. It'll provide backup audio recording in case your boom mic sound or lav mic sound is no good (or is nonexistent because you forgot to hit the "Record" button on your field recorder or Tascams!). This will save your a— many times over the course of shooting. The 9-volt battery it requires will last a long time, but keep one or two backup batteries in your camera bag anyway.

- A slate and markers. Weirdly, slates are expensive. But they make it easy to sync sound in editing and, of course, to slate each take you shoot (with the scene numbers you add to your script using the menu option in Final Draft software). If you don't have the money for one, you'll want to clap loudly on camera right after you hit "Record" when starting to shoot each scene.

- If you cannot afford sound gear or otherwise must use in-camera audio recordings, you often can greatly improve sound quality using the powerful editing tools available in Premiere Pro or other editing platforms. Search "how to fix audio" online to find helpful videos (such as "Massively Improve Your Audio with These 4 Effects in Premiere Pro" from Kevin Fremon on YouTube).

Chapter 9

Directing

I'm sitting here thinking about what I want to say about directing, and the first thing that came to me is this: You know what's awkward? Directing sex scenes.

But we'll get to that in a minute.

Directing encompasses so much. First, it's about choosing an idea or story and committing to bringing it to fruition. You assemble a group of people (however small or big) and lead them toward a vision.

You might wish the job didn't involve being a leader, but there's no getting around it. If you avoid being the leader— if you cede power during production, say, because you don't want to take responsibility for the outcome of all the big and small decisions that must be made—you'll regret it. If you let someone else take the reins, it'll become *their* movie—what they want and what they envision. So, stay in charge the entire journey. Don't let anyone talk you into anything that you don't really want to be part of your film. You can be firm and still be a pleasant person others enjoy collaborating with.

Directing involves making a lot of decisions and some mistakes. Occasionally, when I'm just sitting on my couch thinking about nothing in particular, a memory of some gaffe I made on set will suddenly come to mind. When you leave your comfort zone and engage with other people, good things happen, but also embarrassing things. The best policy is to just accept that you will make mistakes and readily own them when you do. It earns others' respect and trust, and it saves you from trying to hide or point fingers. When I'm working on a project, at least once a day I say, "I fucked up!" Who cares? So what?

From dusk till dawn, you'll be deciding "This shirt or that shirt?" "In the living room or on the patio?" "Should she laugh at the end of that dialogue or just have a hint of a smile?" "Get another take or move on?" There will be endless opportunities to make the wrong call, to not know what you're doing, to make a fool of yourself. One of my favorite quotes about filmmaking is from Werner Herzog: "You are always out of your comfort zone when you are making a film. The whole thing is a journey of humiliation and shame." But you can't let this scare you. The glory of having a finished film is worth it.

Directing involves style and vision. Style is about how we explore the subject matter that interests us—the conscious and unconscious choices we make that give our work its unique tone, look, and feeling. I read somewhere that style = specificity + repetition. Put another way, the motifs or patterns that emerge from our body of work become our style. Vision can be defined as imagination but also "unusual discernment or foresight," according to Merriam-Webster. Directors who are considered vision-aries, whose films have style and are easily distinguishable from others, are often the most celebrated.

Interestingly, according to these definitions, some of my favorite films would not be considered to have extraor-dinary vision or style. They're my favorite usually because the characters are experiencing something that I relate to, that is familiar from my own life, and because I connect to them personally. The films I love that do show vision and have tremendous style, like *All That Jazz*, *Do the Right Thing*, or *Tampopo*, to me would not be worth watching again and again if they did not also ask interesting questions about how to live.

Play Well with Others

Directing is also about learning to work successfully with a variety of personality types, which means you must be or become a good communicator. Like people always say, filmmaking is a collaborative art form. Before I shot my first movie, I wasn't excited about that. I actually wished I didn't have to collaborate with others! I just wanted to rely on myself and no one else. But after wrapping production, I felt completely different. Something magical happens when people gather to do something. Each person contributes cool things you could never have anticipated, and there's a collective sense of awe when you all realize things are going well and you're possibly making something great together.

It's easy to become stressed when you're producing and directing a film. But obviously you don't want to take it out on other people. If you start barking direction at actors, you will create an unpleasant environment where they don't feel safe letting go of their inhibitions and taking creative risks—and your project will suffer. You might also develop a reputation that causes talented people to say no to working with you. It's much better to cultivate a positive atmosphere in which people are inspired to do good work. (This point might seem obvious, yet I know there are some famous directors who don't mind using fear to keep people on their toes.)

Working with Actors

Over time, I've come to think my most important task when directing actors is to make them feel safe and supported. Their work requires them to be vulnerable and brave, and I want them to be completely comfortable taking chances. I also want them to feel valued and appreciated. I admire what they do and I'm grateful for it.

Establishing a good rapport is key, one reason being that it makes it easier for you both to discuss your thoughts and opinions on the characters they'll be playing. At the start of a project, before you begin shooting, you need to find out whether you're on the same page. Sometimes an actor will decide to play a character in a way that surprises you. On my short film, *The Jim Rapke Show*, the lead actor chose to speak in a California surfer patois. At first I was taken aback, but I quickly realized I liked it. If I hadn't agreed with this choice, I would have asked to have a private conversation with him about it, to see if we could land on a different, mutually satisfactory approach.

You Need Good Actors

Like a lot of movie lovers, I have many great performances burned on my brain: Rosanna Arquette's freak-out—"Your chips are cashed!"—in *Nobody's Fool*; Kristen Stewart in *Speak*; Regina King in *Jerry Maguire*; Austin Pendleton in *Starting Over*; Candy Clark in *American Graffiti*; Viola Davis in *Doubt*; Patricia Arquette in *Flirting with Disaster*; Nobuko Miyamoto in *Tampopo*; Michael K. Williams and the whole rest of the cast of *The Wire*. I could go on. Some people just come alive on camera. If you meet an actor who's compelling—known or unknown—and who's game to be in your super-low-budget indie project, cherish them. They will create memorable moments and elevate your work.

My favorite good actors are total pros. They come to set with sometimes 80-plus pages of dialogue memorized, they have the stamina for long days and 17 takes, and often they keep the crew laughing with their riffing on in-jokes that develop during production. When I'm shooting solo, often an actor and I will have such interesting discussions we barely notice we're shooting scenes.

I try to make it clear to the actors I work with how much I value and appreciate them. And I try to work with good ones over and over, which is why you see a lot of the same people in all my projects. People have sometimes commented that it's as if I work with a theater company, and I like that analogy.

Respond to Every Take

You may have heard this: "Casting is 90% of directing." It's true that if you cast the right person for the role, you might not have to do much to get a good performance.

On set, you might find there's an actor in your cast who seems not to need or want much direction from you, and another who prefers or requires frequent communication. But no matter what, it is ideal to address the actors after every take, even if with just a short word of praise or feedback—because the actor(s) will have just done their work and will naturally want to hear what you think. Sometimes your response will be obvious; for example, if their performance made you laugh or cry.

Push for Just One More

There will be times when you're not 100% sure you got what you needed from a take. When you're pressed for time, you might be tempted to just move on. But if you think about it, everything you've done to get to this moment—all of the planning, coordinating, spending—will be for naught if you don't get what you need. So it's worth it to push for one more take. But if you want something different from the actors, be sure to give them a new intention to play (more about this below), even if it's only slightly different from a prior intention.

Sometimes Tradition is Best

I once read about a successful TV showrunner who was famous for their sensitive touch with actors. As part of their approach to fostering a nurturing environment on set, instead of yelling, "ACTION!" they would just gently inform the actors that they could "Begin." So, the next time I was on set, I tried something similar. Instead of saying, "ACTION!" I just quietly told the actors, "The camera is rolling." And what I found is that the actors were confused about whether we had really begun. Finally one of them asked me if I could just go back to calling out, "ACTION!" So I did.

Shooting Out of Order

If you're shooting scenes out of order, which most actors are used to doing (actually, I think it's rarer to shoot a script in order), just remind the actors where they are in the story and what their character is experiencing at that point in their emotional arc.

Table Reads and Rehearsals

I've not yet been motivated to schedule rehearsal time with actors because it's hard enough scheduling time to shoot with them. There are directors and actors I admire who feel rehearsal time is critical and just as many who say they prefer not to rehearse. I of course see the potential value in rehearsing and would be interested in doing it if the actors wanted to and if I were able to pay everyone for their time. At the minimum, when you're loading in your gear and setting up to shoot, your actors will probably want to run lines with each other in another room or, if you're outdoors, in a quiet spot just yards away. But either a table read or a proper rehearsal before beginning production can be useful for helping the actors get comfortable with their dialogue, seeing whether there are any lines they find awkward to deliver (and which you might want to revise), learning whether there is any confusion about aspects of the story, and perhaps most importantly for you, discovering whether you are comfortable with how they intend to portray the characters. But you can and should do all of these things whether or not you have a table read or rehearsal period.

Directing Sex Scenes

As I mentioned at the start, what I find most uncomfortable is shooting sex scenes. Even though you "only" have to shoot the scene in such a way that it appears the actors are doing something sexual even though they're not really, it's still tricky. If you've read anything about this topic, then you probably already know you should clear the set as much as possible, allowing only the most necessary crew members to be present. Easy to do when you shoot solo! But still, there is the question of what to *say* to the actors and how to direct them. I think what I said to Mike Friedman and Cate Beehan Russo in *What Other Couples Do* was, "Uh, just act like you're doing it?" (I know. Ridiculous.) Maybe you're more emotionally mature than I am and find it easy to speak in explicit terms about how to pretend to have sex. Even so, another concern is making sure the actors feel safe and comfortable. But guess what? I recently discovered there's a solution for these issues: an intimacy coordinator!

An intimacy coordinator is a trained professional who helps choreograph sex or intimacy scenes and who ensures actors are treated with respect and are safe during rehearsal and shooting of the scenes. This is a relatively new job title but these coordinators/choreographers should have been present on sets since the advent of filmmaking. I hate wondering how many actors have been violated on set because no one was present to provide oversight during the shooting of sex or intimacy scenes. I look forward to hiring a certified intimacy coordinator the next time I shoot a sex scene.

Shooting Big Emotional Scenes

When shooting a scene, I don't want actors to feel any pressure to "nail it." Especially when it comes to a big emotional scene. It's exhilarating when an actor gives a great performance, and of course I celebrate it. But I don't want anyone going into a scene thinking they "must" cry or deliver some other specific behavior. What matters is whether their performance causes me to *feel* something.

Right before we shot the emotional climax of *Bedroom Story*, I told the lead actress, Annie Cavalero, there was no pressure to "cry uncontrollably" like I'd written in the script. I told the lead actor, Mike Friedman, that he didn't have to "explode" from pent-up anger, which I'd also written in the script. Even though I was privately half hoping she would indeed cry and he would "explode," I wanted to let go of my expectations and embrace whatever happened—which turned out to be better than I had imagined. To this day, I can barely watch that scene in the finished film because it's so uncomfortable. Annie and Mike were so effective, I remember having a hard time staying present mentally and physically during the shooting of it. I had to restrain myself from dashing out of the room every take!

The Keys to a Natural Performance

What I typically say to actors right before we roll camera is this: I ask them to please forget themselves as much as possible and focus on their scene partner. I remind them to really *listen* to their partner. If they do this, there's a good chance they'll be less self-conscious and more natural. I learned this from renowned acting coach Judith Weston's invaluable book, *Directing Actors: 25th Anniversary Edition*:

> "Actors have this secret weapon: *another actor.* For a baseline of believability and presence, surrendering to a scene partner is the safe and reliable place for actors. The technique is this: the actor puts more attention on his acting partner than on his own performance."[4]

And she says listening is the key to great performances:

> "When the actors are actively listening to each other, it not only makes the acting natural and real, it allows the actors to affect each other, and thus to create *moments*—tiny electric connections that happen *in real time* and make the scene work."[5]

---

4 Weston, 57.

5 Weston, 59.

Use Action Verbs, Not Adjectives

When you shoot a scene and it doesn't work, you might pause for a few minutes and discuss with the actors what is happening in the scene, what the subtext of the scene is, what the audience needs to take away from the scene, and/or how the scene will impact the trajectory of the story.

Before you shoot another take, try giving the actors an intention, which is basically a goal for the scene. It's best to do this with action verbs. Action verbs give the actors something specific to play. For example, you might ask one of the actors to "seduce" their scene partner, or "threaten" their partner, or "punish" their partner.

It's common for inexperienced directors to give actors adjectives to play. For example, when you're just starting out, the natural thing to do is tell an actor to "act sad," or "be happy." But if you put yourself in the actor's shoes, you'll realize how difficult it would be to proceed with this kind of direction. If you try to "act sad," you might feel like you're just miming. Attempting to perform an emotion or attitude can be awkward and cringe-inducing. Consider how much more helpful it is to be given a specific action verb to play. Saying your lines with an intention to, for instance, "flirt with your scene partner" is much easier than trying to "act sexy."

It's been said that every scene is either a fight, a negotiation, or a seduction. So, if in the heat of the moment (i.e., while shooting), you are only able to remember these three action-verb directions—"Fight them," "Negotiate with them," or "Seduce them"—you might get by.

An Emotional Event Must Occur

As Weston observes:

> **"If one character is *begging* and the other is *ridiculing*, something will happen! Someone will get hurt—or won over—or maybe something else no one expected. These are the *emotional events.*"[6]**

It's crucial that an emotional event occurs in every scene. If not, the scene will probably just lie there, lifeless, and you'll likely have to cut it. Or you'll wish you could! I've been in this situation a few times. Don't think I blame the actors—it's never their fault. If I don't get a good performance, it's my fault.

---

6 Weston, 15.

Set Yourself Up for Success

I think directing has something in common with breast-feeding. I've heard that many women assume breast-feeding will come naturally to them, but evidently most encounter some difficulty when getting started and end up needing to educate themselves and/or get some support or guidance. Directing is the same. You might assume it'll come naturally to you, but it's more likely that you'll need some education and guidance.

If you read only one book devoted to the subject, read Weston's. She used to lead popular acting workshops for directors, and there are a lot of testimonials from famous directors saying how revelatory it was to work with her and experience what actors experience. Her book is a thorough, incredibly helpful exploration of every topic relevant to directing actors. When you skim the table of contents, there's so much gold hinted at, you'll be eager to dive in.

Every time you shoot, there will be moments when you'll struggle to express what you want from the actors. If you read Weston's book, you'll be so much better prepared to communicate effectively with them and get good, if not great, performances from them.

Chapter 10

Production

To me, the absolute best thing about owning gear (as opposed to renting it for a limited time period or borrowing it from a friend) and working solo is that you don't have to have a super intense production period composed of 14-hour days—unless you want to!

Instead, when you shoot solo, you can have balance in your life. You can get good sleep, you can walk your dogs, you can have a life. To the uninitiated, this may be underwhelming. But anyone who has worked on a film knows that production is no joke. Especially when it's your movie and you are wearing many hats (directing, producing, script supervising, etc.).

Shooting solo is even easier and more laid back if you have relatively easy access to the location(s) you'll be using. For this reason, I try to shoot in my own home as much as possible. I've shot in every corner of my house, as well as in my backyard, at my front door, and on my driveway.

If your actors want to be free to go on auditions and otherwise tend to their lives, you can shoot in one-, two-, and three-hour chunks, grabbing scenes day in and day out or working only every couple of days, depending on what is most convenient for them and you.

However, keep in mind that if you're *too* lax about shooting, you run the risk of continuity problems: people's hairstyles change, they gain and lose weight, they age...or worse, they sometimes decide to quit acting and move out of state! So, you do want to be fairly disciplined about it. But it's nice not having to work almost nonstop for two or three weeks straight.

Whether you're down with this "Just bag scenes at a civilized pace" guideline, or if you find this approach too vague, recall that you can read Ralph S. Singleton's *Film Scheduling* to learn how to break down a script and schedule a shoot in a professional, methodical way. You don't have to do everything the book suggests, but it provides a great education, it's actually very interesting, and you can pick and choose the parts you want to adhere to.

Shooting Your Script (a.k.a. "Production")

Below are my top production tips, most of which I learned the hard way (by making many mistakes!). Following these guidelines will save you a lot of headaches.

- Add scene numbers to your script using the menu option in Final Draft or whichever screenwriting software you use. Each time you shoot, bring a hard copy of the scene pages you'll be shooting that day. Before you shoot each take, write the scene and take number on your film slate. This will help you stay organized for the editing phase.

- Search "actor release form" online, print as many copies as you'll need for the number of actors you'll be shooting with (plus an extra copy or two for unexpected walk-ons), and obtain signatures on set. Or download a film production app that includes actor release forms and get electronic signatures from your actors before you shoot.

- You'll be carrying your gear from your house to your car and from your car to your actors' homes or whatever locations you're using. So keep it well-organized and pared down to only the items you really use. If you have various lighting tools—China balls, Quasars, etc.—see if you can put them in a big lightweight bag, plastic bin, or other transportable vessel.

- ABC: Always Be Charging. Make sure all your camera batteries are fully charged before you leave the house. If they are completely drained, it'll take two to three hours or more to charge each, so check them the day before your shoot. The ideal is to start charging a battery immediately after it's depleted so that it's available to you as soon as possible if you end up needing it.

- Make sure there's a blank camera card in your camera and an extra in your camera bag. When you've been transferring footage from a card to your computer, it's easy to leave the card in your computer and forget all about it until you get to a shoot location and realize your card is at home! So here's a "best practices" set of steps to follow:

    1. Save new footage to your desktop or laptop computer immediately after shooting.

    2. Eject the memory card, then make sure the footage from the card is in fact saved onto your computer (open it to see).

    3. Put the memory card back into your camera, then choose the "Format" menu option and delete the footage from the card so that it's empty and ready to store new footage at the next shoot.

- Bring my shooting checklist or your own, so that you remember everything you need to do before hitting "Record" on the camera. When you first start shooting solo, you will be juggling a lot of tasks that are new to you, so keeping track of everything will be challenging. I'd print out the checklist, bring it with you to set, place it on the floor next to your feet and tripod, and glance at it before starting to shoot.

- If you'll be shooting for more than an hour, bring a snack or meal for yourself and your actor(s), and bring a refillable water bottle.

- Make sure your cell phone is charged before you head to the shoot.

- If you don't own a monitor and you'd like to check the footage you're getting on a bigger screen than your camera's display, bring your charged laptop computer and a memory card reader (if your computer doesn't have an SD card reader port) to shoots.

- Transport all your gear in the trunk of your car so that it's not visible to passersby if you stop anywhere on the way to or from the shoot, and be sure to lock your car.

- Consider getting insurance coverage for your gear if you cannot afford to replace it if something were to happen to it.

- Ask your cast to bring at least a couple of options from their own wardrobe to every shoot. Or, if one or more of the actors wears the same size as you or your spouse, partner or best friend, shop your own closet or theirs to provide wardrobe options.

Shooting Checklist

You might want to copy and print out the following list and keep it in your camera bag. When you arrive on location, you can take it out and set it on the ground next to your tripod. Glance at it as you set up your gear, then skim all of it again before you hit "Record."

The day before you shoot:

- Charge the batteries for your camera as well as your lighting tools.

- Pack extra batteries for sound recording gear.

- Pack actor release forms and a copy of the script pages you'll be shooting.

- Transfer any footage from your camera memory card to your computer. Double-check the footage is on your computer. Put the card back in your camera and "format" it (delete the files you just transferred to your computer).

- Check your camera's battery levels.

- Charge your laptop computer and pack it and a memory card reader, if desired.

Day of shoot:

- At an indoor shoot, before bringing in any gear, choose a spot that's not in the way of foot traffic and lay down a canvas drop cloth to protect the floor.

- Before setting up your camera, choose where the actor will stand or sit in the shot. Usually you'll want to take

advantage of available natural light (such as shooting
near a window, if indoors; if outdoors on a bright day,
you might want to look for a slightly shaded spot to
avoid harsh overhead sun). Assess the light and how it
falls on the actor. If there's a hot spot on their face or
head, or if there are distracting reflections of light
dancing around on their face, make tweaks to see if you
can solve the issue (partially close the curtains or blinds
on a window, turn the actor away from the window or
light source slightly, move to a shadier spot, use your
neutral density filter, etc.). If the spot you chose is not
working, find another.

- When you know where you're shooting, set up your
  tripod, turn on your camera (and monitor, if you have
  one) and frame the shot.

- If you're already using a wide-open aperture (such as
  f/2.8) and you don't have added lighting to work with
  and must use ISO to let in more light, here are typical
  ISO settings for specific situations:

  - Sunny: 100
  - Partly cloudy: 200
  - Overcast: 400
  - Indoors: 800
  - Very dark lighting: 1600
  - Dark/night: 3200-6400

- If you feel comfortable reading a false color scope, look
  at yours to see if there are any areas of the shot in
  which whites are clipped (100 IRE; possibly represented
  by the color red) or blacks are crushed (0 IRE; possibly
  represented by deep purple). Adjust the lighting, adjust
  your aperture or ISO, use an ND filter, or otherwise
  change the variables until there is no area of your shot
  that is completely overexposed or underexposed.

- If you have practiced achieving specific lighting looks (using a light meter or the false color scope on your monitor), make adjustments to the lighting to get the contrast ratio you want.

- Before recording a test shot or your first take, check to make sure the framing is flattering to the actor(s). Is there enough headroom? Are any of their limbs being chopped at an awkward spot? Is there a door frame, potted plant, or other item in the background "growing out of their head" or otherwise creating a weird shot? How does their hair look? Are there any strands out of place that will be distracting to the viewer?

- Look at the background and set decor through the viewfinder or on your monitor. Fix or remove anything that is distracting.

- Turn on your camera's shotgun mic to record backup audio.

- If you're using lav mics, record test dialogue and listen to it to make sure there's no crackling or clothing rustling noise. Make sure the lav mic wires are completely hidden from view when the actors put the recorders in their pockets.

- Record several seconds of test dialogue on your boom mic field recorder and set the gain to -12 dB. Check the playback. Raise the gain if needed. Hit "Record" again, look at the display to make sure it's recording, attach the recorder to your boom pole, and place the pole in its cradle (an Auray boom stand or other brand) on a C-stand. Position the mic so that it's just above the top of the frame, about 12–18 inches away from the actor and aimed at a 45-degree angle to their mouth or chin.

- Get custom white balance. If you use an 18% gray dome or card to do this, be sure to remove it from the scene.

Set the white balance every time you change the
lighting or move locations.

- Look at the histogram to see if the exposure is decent
(not climbing the left or right walls of the graph), or get
more detailed exposure information by looking at the
false color scope, if you feel comfortable reading one.

- Ask your host to turn off the AC/heat and unplug any
appliances that create noise, even if only a low hum.
Some people put their car keys in the fridge so that they
remember to plug the fridge back in before they leave.

- When you are ready to shoot your first take, hit the
"Record" button on your camera, announce the scene or
scene number you're shooting, and use a slate or clap
loudly in front of the camera.

- If possible, play back each take you shoot, to make sure
you got it.

- Turn the camera off every chance you get to help
prevent it overheating. (I once shot for hours in a small
bathroom on a hot day, my camera overheated, and the
last take I shot did not survive—it looked like it had been
recorded, but when I tried to watch it in playback, there
was only a "?" graphic in place of that take.)

- After you stop recording a take, hit the "Stop" button on
your boom mic recorder (rather than the "Pause" button).
If there tends to be a lot of time between your takes, turn
off your camera immediately after you stop recording,
to save battery power and help prevent overheating.

- After shooting a scene, record at least one minute of
room tone.

- Remind your host to turn on the AC/heat or any appliances that were turned off for the shoot.

- As you break down and load out your gear, be careful not to knock into or scratch anything with your C-stands and tripod.

- Send payment to the actors using Venmo or whatever method is mutually agreeable.

Chapter 11

Post-Production

Post-production usually takes 3–6 months but sometimes longer. On *Bedroom Story*, my wonderful editor, Jason Barnoski, got the dailies every night and was able to work full time on the first cut of the film. I was lucky enough to see a quite polished draft of the film within a month of wrapping production. Even so, we still sat together discussing and making little revisions over multiple editing sessions to get to the final draft of the film.

With *This Fucking Town*, I made rough cuts of each scene immediately after shooting the footage. Then, whenever I was not writing or shooting, I would return to editing and make each rough cut a little smoother.

While editing your film, you'll be sourcing music, adding opening and end credits, adding sound effects, working with a graphic designer or designing a poster yourself, gathering any good production stills or screenshots from key moments in the film (to upload as part of your "assets" if you distribute the film through an aggregator like Filmhub), and fulfilling remaining SAG obligations if yours was a SAG production. You can imagine how busy this keeps you, for weeks or months, while you get your film to the finish line.

Learn Just Enough to Edit

Having footage in the can reminds me of being a kid on Halloween, coming home from trick-or-treating and dumping all the candy I bagged onto my bed. Editing is where you pore over all the "candy" you got and decide what portions of your footage you want to use, where to enter a scene and when to exit it, what to emphasize—whether people, places, or objects—and how slow or fast you want the pacing of your film to be.

As with cinematography, editing is its own craft and there is of course no substitute for getting years of practice to become great. But learning even just basic editing skills is incredibly empowering. It is so gratifying to be able to put together a rough cut right after shooting new footage. Think of it—rather than just sitting on your hands, waiting for an editor to work on your project, you can immediately see what you've got!

When I wanted to learn how to edit, I asked friends and editors what platform they recommended. I kept hearing good things about Adobe Premiere Pro. So, that's the program I learned and still use. I love it. I've found it fairly intuitive and relatively easy to learn. After less than an hour of taking a beginner course in it, I was already putting together a rough cut of a video. If I can do that, I know you can, too.

Some tips for learning how to edit:

- If you're interested in using Premiere Pro, go to Adobe. com and pay for a subscription. Individual app plans (i.e., for Premiere Pro only) are $9.99/month. The Creative Cloud All Apps plan is $54.99/month and enables you to use Photoshop, Lightroom, etc. as well as Adobe's cloud storage.

- Go to LinkedIn Learning online, sign up for a free month's trial, and take a beginner's course in Premiere Pro or whatever editing software program you've chosen to learn. I really like Ashley Kennedy's videos. She offers a beginner's course in editing called "Introduction to Video Editing" as well as a course called "Premiere Pro 2022 Essential Training."

- Be sure to mark a date on your calendar that is just under a month away, reminding yourself to cancel your subscriptions to both Adobe and LinkedIn Learning if you don't end up liking editing or if you are otherwise not using your subscriptions.

- Search "transitions in film editing" on YouTube to learn basics such as how to dissolve, fade, cross cut, match cut, etc.

- Search "best audio effects in Premiere Pro" (or whatever editing software you're using) to learn how to use cool tools such as the "denoise" filter to get rid of background noise, the high pass filter for phone conversations, etc.

- Learn what legendary editors have to say. Search "Thelma Schoonmaker on editing" to find interviews in which the three-time Academy Award winner shares her thoughts on "blender cutting," test screenings, and working on Scorsese's films for the past 40 years. Search "film editor Dede Allen," who was a sound editor before cutting *Bonnie and Clyde*, *The Hustler*, *Serpico*, *Dog Day Afternoon*, *Let It Ride*, *The Breakfast Club*, and *Wonder Boys*, to find out how she changed filmmaking during her 60-year career. Read *In the Blink of an Eye* by

Walter Murch, editor of *American Graffiti*, *The Godfather II* and *III*, and *Apocalypse Now*, to learn his "rule of 6" criteria for what makes a good cut. He explains what the blinking of an actor's eyes has to do with the rhythm and pacing of a film, how he chooses the "out" point of a shot, what film editing has in common with bumblebees and the DNA of humans and chimpanzees, and why film is more like thought than any other art form. Both deep and accessible, it's a great book. Study the work of British editor Anne V. Coates (*Lawrence of Arabia*, *Out of Sight*, and David Lynch's *The Elephant Man*), Sally Menke (edited all of Quentin Tarantino's films until she passed in 2010, Oscar-nominated for *Pulp Fiction* and *Inglourious Basterds*), and Joi McMillon (editor of Barry Jenkins' beautiful film, *If Beale Street Could Talk*, and the first Black woman editor to be nominated for an Oscar).

Know Your Footage Well

Before you make a single cut, the first thing you should do is watch all your footage as many times as you can stand to (at least twice, but ideally more than twice). As you become familiar with it, you'll start to develop a preference for certain takes or specific moments within takes. Make notes, including timecodes, in an editing log (either a spiral notebook or pad of paper, or a document on your computer).

Most importantly, you'll start to see possible paths to take through the forest, so to speak.

When you wrote the script for your film, you might have told your story in a straightforward way. In editing, you might decide to give your story a non-linear structure. For example, you might decide that a scene originally written to take place near the end of the story would be more impactful if placed at the beginning of the film. That's what's cool about editing—it allows so much creativity.

Besides experimenting with placing scenes out of chronological order, you might want to try the following:

- Repeat certain moments to see if it heightens emotion.

- Linger on a shot to make the viewer think more about the subtext of the scene.

- Make jump cuts to quicken the pace.

- Use insert shots to show a person's thoughts flitting from one image or memory to another.

- String together snippets from multiple scenes to create a montage.

- Add VO (voiceover) to provide narration, clarification, or commentary.

- Place two characters' dialogue over a shot of something else (i.e., don't show the characters at all for that scene).

- Use music or a soundscape for emotional effect or to maximize conflict. For example, try eerie or discordant music or a discomfiting noise (such as the howling, drone-like wind in David Lynch's *Eraserhead*) to create dread or tension.

While editing, if you find that your story is not coming together, consider the possibility of shooting more footage, to fill in gaps or even to push it in a whole new direction.

Cutting Patterns

If you shot a lot of coverage for a particular scene, you'll probably find yourself wondering what your cutting pattern should be. Start with a wide establishing shot, then cut to a medium close-up, then an extreme close-up, then back to the wide? OR, start with an extreme close-up, then cut to a wide shot, then a medium close-up...? You get the idea. This is just one of the reasons I hate having lots of coverage—too many options! But more importantly, it's boring filmmaking to have too many scenes that play out in some version of the patterns I just described. You might want to mix things up by limiting yourself to just a couple of camera angles for some scenes.

But back to which shot to start a scene with. I sometimes think that starting on a wide and holding off on showing a closer shot of a character can make the viewer more eager to see them, more eager to "get close." It can add mystery and tension. On the other hand, going from the previous scene straight to a close-up of a character's face can be dramatic and impactful. (For some reason, I don't shoot many extreme close-ups of actors. I don't know why. Certainly there are uses for an extreme close-up of a character. Maybe ECUs feel invasive, or too intimate, to me? Perhaps this is a topic to discuss with my therapist.) Beyond this advice, I think you should let emotion dictate which shots to use—for example, if a particular take evokes the most emotion from you when watching it, then you should stay in that shot as much as possible. What I usually do is cherry-pick the best moments from each take and see if the resulting cutting pattern flows smoothly.

Sound Can Sell It

Remember that the sound in a movie is hugely important. (How important? Walter Murch spent a year editing the picture for *Apocalypse Now* and another year editing the sound.) As you work on your film, always be asking yourself what you can do to the audio to make each scene more impactful and convincing. For example, use L and J cuts to make a phone conversation more dynamic and seamless, rather than lingering on each person until they've finished speaking (Google "J and L cuts in filmmaking" for details, but essentially, it involves cutting from person A to person B before person A has finished speaking—i.e., the audio for person A is still playing while you've cut to the video of person B listening or reacting—and then when person B speaks, you cut back to video of person A before person B has finished speaking).

Put a piece of the room tone you recorded for a scene under an entire sequence to make the cuts to different takes smoother. Learn how to use a high pass filter (or the "from the telephone" preset, if you're using Premiere Pro) to make audio sound like it's coming through a phone. Take the time to add ambient noise such as birds chirping, traffic passing on the street, background chatter, or other sounds from real life, when appropriate, to make a scene more believable. You can choose from the library of free sound effects in Audition (which is included in an Adobe Creative Cloud subscription) or search "royalty-free sound effects" online.

If your sound needs a lot of work and you have the budget for it, consider hiring a sound editor.

Learn Cool Tricks as You Go

I'm still always surprised at how easy it is to learn anything you could want to do in editing. Just enter a topic in your search engine—say, "How to correct skin color," or "How to color match footage," or "How to correct white balance"—and you'll find concise, easy to follow tutorials from your editing software maker (helpxAdobe.com if you're using Premiere Pro) or short videos from YouTube pros who show you their editing screen as they demonstrate techniques and tools. You don't need to try to memorize all the things you learn. You can always go find a good tutorial again when the need arises. The important thing to realize is that there is almost always a way to improve, if not solve, any issue with your footage in editing.

Opening and End Credits

You can create title cards for your opening credits and an end credits crawl (scrolling text) for your film in Premiere Pro and other film editing software programs. Search the topic online to find instructions or a YouTube tutorial. When you're typing in the names of your collaborators to create the credits, even if you feel positive you know how to spell everyone's names, get confirmation from each person.

Great Music is Key

I once read a *New Yorker* article in which film editors, working with a test audience, tried several different music cues for what the filmmakers hoped was an emotionally impactful scene. Everyone had watched the scene, accompanied by different bits of music, about 20 times, and no one had shed a tear. When the editors finally landed on the right song, everyone cried.

It was either in that article or elsewhere that I read a quote that I mentioned earlier in this book: "People don't watch a movie, they listen to a movie." Obviously, music has the power to affect people deeply. Getting good music for your movie is key.

To control costs, don't attempt to make music licensing deals with, say, 10 different bands. Making offers and then negotiating with bands' or musicians' reps is time-consuming and ends up being expensive. Even when you have a direct "in" to a band, you almost always end up having to go through their manager or publisher to pay for sync and publishing licenses.

A much simpler, more affordable approach is to work with a composer who is willing to provide an original score for an affordable rate, either because they like your project or because they are looking to add credits to their resume.

Hybrid approach: pay for an original score, plus obtain the license to use one song from a band whose rep will let you have it for an affordable price.

If you have no referrals from friends for a composer, search for film composers online. Looking for potential collaborators on Instagram can be good because you can usually get a sense of a person's personality, taste, and sensibilities by looking at their feed.

Hire a Pro

If you don't have the patience or time to become good at editing, or even if you are a decent editor but are unhappy with your movie, hire a professional. A great editor can make the difference between having an unwatchable hot mess to having a film that you actually like or even love.

Chapter 12

Distribution— A Cautionary Tale

Instead of telling you what I think you should do with your finished film, I'm going to tell you what I did with my second feature, *Bedroom Story*, and you can form your own takeaway.

Film Festivals

When we finished the movie, my editor Jason Barnoski and I had lunch in his neighborhood to discuss it. We talked about the fact that the film is small—it's character-driven, the entire story takes place in a couple's bedroom, and there are no stars in the cast. He thought the chances of it being selected by a big festival were slim and I agreed. He had just read a book about the punk rock movement and observed that what *we* were doing was punk—i.e., making things truly independently, outside of the studio system. He felt we should stay on our indie path and forget about the establishment route (arguably the festival landscape is a microcosm of the studio value system). After my experience with *What Other Couples Do*, in which I entered a lot of festivals and was accepted by only one, I didn't have high expectations this time around. Jason thought we should just release the movie online, immediately. We were excited about getting it out into the world because we thought it might resonate with people.

In my heart, that's what I wanted to do—release *Bedroom Story* online, immediately. But my head said "no." I wondered how the actors would feel if they heard I hadn't submitted it to a single festival. The logical, rational part of me thought I should be patient, take the long view, and try again to get the validation and exposure that could move the needle on everyone's careers. So I decided I would submit the film to just a few of the big festivals that were coming up that fall. And I would try to get a distribution deal.

An independent film industry veteran had told me that it's almost futile to make a blind submission to a festival.[7] They said that the most prestigious festivals, in particular, rarely select such films. Knowing this, I submitted to a few festivals anyway, hoping against hope that my movie would get seen.

At the last minute, right before their late deadline, I also submitted the film to my favorite festival, the one that had screened *What Other Couples Do*—the Pasadena International Film Festival (PIFF). I had heard it's foolish to submit to a festival at the eleventh hour because of the likelihood that the festival programmers had already committed to a lineup. At any rate, they passed on my movie. So did all the other festivals I'd submitted to.

---

7 A blind submission is one in which there has been no contact between the filmmaker or their team and the festival (i.e., the filmmaker has no connections at the festival, and no one at the festival has been tracking their film or anticipating its arrival).

Sales Reps, Distributors, Licensing, and Aggregators

Shortly after I received Pasadena's rejection notice, I got an email from a film sales rep who said he was on the short film judging panel there and that one of the festival directors had told him *Bedroom Story* was a standout. He asked if I would be game to let him see the movie. He watched it, said it was "terrific," and told me about his services. I paid his fee ($3,500), I paid to have Blu-ray copies made of my movie ($1,000), he sent them to approximately 25 reputable distributors, and we waited for their response.

Two months passed. Then we received an offer from a distributor whose name was familiar to me because I had seen their logo in film credits. The offer was not tempting. Here were the terms: The distributor would get 30% of profits, the sales agent would get 5%, and the distributor would own the rights to the film for 20 years.

Before I could decide whether to pass on the offer, I had some questions for the distributor. In a phone conversation, I asked him what the odds were of the movie being licensed by Netflix. Not great, he said. Years ago, Netflix licensed a lot of films from companies like his. But now that they are creating a lot of original content, they are prioritizing promotion of those films and shows over other content. And when they do promote other content, it's movies and shows that feature stars and name actors. I believe he said it was the same with the big cable streamers like HBO and Showtime.

Then I asked him: If we did happen to get licensed by one of those sites, what were the chances of viewers discovering the movie? Would it be recommended to target audiences, or would it be a needle in a haystack? Answer: Needle in a haystack. That is, unless it goes viral, in which case the algorithm would be triggered to show it to more potential viewers. But even then, you don't get a percentage of royalties. Instead, you get a flat fee (which I've heard is modest) upfront when they license a film, usually for a period of one year or a maximum of three years.

I then asked him what the plan was for the film if it didn't get picked up by Netflix or cable streamers. He said they would release it on TVOD sites (transactional video on demand, in which viewers must pay to rent or buy the film) for a certain window of time (say, six months, or until sales dwindle), then release it on AVOD sites (advertising video on demand, in which viewers can watch the movie for free but agree to be shown ads, which is how the site monetizes the exchange), where it would presumably live for a while (longer than six months).

At this point, I should mention that a rep at Filmhub (the online aggregator[8] who distributes my first film, *What Other Couples Do*) had already informed me that most viewers will not take the risk of paying out of pocket (TVOD) to see a small movie with an unknown cast. However, something like 80% of Americans are open to watching a movie with ads (AVOD). He said, in fact, that TVOD was on its way down and AVOD was on its way up. They were seeing tremendous growth in advertising-monetized streaming.

So, if my movie were released by the distributor, it seemed possible that the only revenue could end up coming from AVOD. Since I could put my movie on certain

---

8 An aggregator is a company that helps you distribute your project by taking it to multiple platforms.

AVOD sites (like Amazon) myself, or use Filmhub to put it on as many AVOD sites as possible, giving them 20% of the royalties (vs. 35%)—and keeping the rights to my film—I declined the offer from the distributor.

At this point, a year had passed since my lunch with Jason. And I was down $4,500.

I had pretty much decided to go with Filmhub again, but I still wanted to see if I could make more than just pennies per stream on Amazon.

Though I knew very well that perhaps not a large percentage of the population is in the habit of going to Vimeo (a TVOD site) for entertainment content, I like the site and decided to release the movie there before signing on with Filmhub. I knew sales would drop off after the first month or so, and I vowed to myself that I would do everything possible to keep driving traffic there. The reasons I like Vimeo: You can set the rental and purchase prices yourself and Vimeo can't change them (like Amazon can), and instead of making just 6–12 cents per stream like you do on Amazon, you make whatever you set as your rental or purchase price minus 10% for Vimeo's cut. Plus, Vimeo has an aesthetically pleasing interface and very reliable streaming bandwidth.

After the first month, in which my friends and family all went to the site to watch my movie, sales did in fact dwindle to almost nothing—as did my determination to drive traffic to the site. Like a lot of creative people, I'm interested in making things, not promoting them. (I know, I know. You *have* to. Believe me, I get it!)

I briefly considered using a different aggregator than Filmhub to release my film. There are a couple other services that will submit your movie to iTunes and Amazon only, for example, or to a few other additional platforms if you want. iTunes requires filmmakers to go through a quality control check at one of their approved labs. For example, Bitmax handles this process for you (for around $1,000), and they offer an option in which those who are short on cash can pay less if they give Bitmax a percentage of the profits. But with *What Other Couples Do*, almost no revenue comes from iTunes, for this reason given by my rep at Filmhub: Most people won't pay money out of pocket to take a chance on a small film with no stars in the cast. But they will take a chance if it's free, such as on Amazon Freevee or Tubi.

In the end, I released *Bedroom Story* with Filmhub. They submit clients' films to more than 50 sites, and they are always adding more platforms. Although some sites' payouts are better than others, Filmhub's strategy is to put your films anywhere and everywhere customers might stumble upon them. Whoever wants your film can add it to their catalog, and you receive royalties after Filmhub takes 20%. You maintain ownership of the rights to your film, and you can depart at any time.

If you prefer that your film only be on sites where it'll make the most money, such as Amazon and Tubi—i.e., if you don't care about it being discoverable on as many platforms as possible—you might want to see whether Amazon is currently allowing filmmakers to submit their films themselves (without an aggregator as intermediary).

Amazon Prime and Freevee

Before committing to Filmhub, I debated submitting the movie to Amazon Prime myself, to save the 20% in royalties I'd pay Filmhub. Since Amazon is where *What Other Couples Do* has made nearly all its revenue, I figured that would be the case with *Bedroom Story*, too. As I mentioned earlier, Amazon reserves the right to change the prices you set for your film's rental and purchase (my guess is that it usually lowers the prices, probably to $1.99 and $2.99–$3.99, respectively, for movies in my category). But this ends up being a moot point, because you'll probably make almost no revenue from rentals or purchases of your movie. If your movie does well on Prime, Amazon will then add it to the Freevee library (content that's free for people who have a subscription to Prime), so your revenue will likely mostly come from this audience.

The bulk of the revenue for both *What Other Couples Do* and *Bedroom Story* comes from Amazon Freevee. Both films started on Prime, then were selected for inclusion in the Freevee library. I've been told the payout for Freevee is a little better than on Prime, but I don't know by how much.

Just because Amazon has insane traffic and there are over a hundred million Prime subscribers doesn't mean your movie will get seen a lot there. There is a mountain of content on Amazon and on every other streaming platform, so it may be that people never find your movie. Even if people do find it, it will have to be seen by a *ton* of people to make a decent amount of money—because filmmakers receive literally pennies per stream. The last I heard, Amazon pays between 6–12 cents. The reason it's a range is because payout is prorated based on the amount of time watched...I think. Don't take my word for any of this—do your own research to find out what you can.

An example of earnings on Amazon Freevee: If you use an aggregator like Filmhub to distribute your movie, after they've taken 20% of royalties, 20,000 streams of your movie might earn you about $1,600 net.

If you find this number underwhelming, I feel you. The payout on many platforms is even lower.

In the past, I considered buying ads on Facebook and Instagram to drive traffic to my movie. But interestingly, the cost-per-customer conversion is almost definitely going to be greater than the tiny payout you get per stream on AVOD platforms. You can of course decide to buy ads anyway, if you are more interested in exposure than anything else. And who knows, maybe the more people know about your film, the more word of mouth will spread, and eventually sales will exceed ad spends. I wouldn't count on this, but it's possible.

In the end, the hope is that you've made a film that people like enough to want to share with friends. Word-of-mouth recommendations are arguably the best way for your movie to travel and continue to be seen for years to come.

Conclusion: Yes You Can

At this point, you might be feeling queasy about all the things you have to tackle to make a film. Your mind might start drifting to fantasies of being picked—i.e., someone in the studio system or some other powerful entity choosing you, giving you financing, and making everything easy. Not only is this not going to happen (okay, there's a chance it could happen; I leave it to you to determine the statistical probability), you don't want it to happen. Here's why:

It's really satisfying to make a movie yourself, with no executives giving you notes and no financiers making the rules. You don't want to be supervised or strong-armed into anything you feel would not be good for your film. It is a major high to be in pure creation mode, with no one telling you what to do or how to do it.

Yes, it'll be challenging. But think about this:

What are you most proud of in your life?

My guess is it's the things that were the hardest to do, accomplish, or overcome. Doing hard things doesn't just make us proud, it makes our lives full and rewarding. Going to the edge of our abilities and finding out what we can accomplish is of course often humbling, but it's also exciting.

Motivational speaker Les Brown says, "If you always do easy things, your life will be hard. If you always do hard things, your life will be easy."

Making a movie is hard. But it won't kill you. And a lot of the time it'll be really fun!

I promise if you make a movie, it'll be one of the things in your life you're most proud of.

If you read this book just because you were curious, great! I hope you found it interesting. If you read this book because you really, really want to make a movie, I hope you go for it. I'm with you in spirit!

Courtney

Gear Shopping List

- Used or new full-frame mirrorless camera that offers a film-like shooting mode of 24fps (such as the Sony a7R V, the a7S IV, or a used a7S III)

- Used or new zoom lens (such as a 24-70mm)

- Neutral density (ND) filter in the size appropriate for your camera lens

- Camera bag with padded compartments for camera body and lens(es) (such as a Peak Design Sling or other bag)

- A study, quality tripod (used or new from Manfrotto or another quality brand)

- At least 2 extra camera batteries, or as many as 6

- At least 2 extra camera memory card(s)

- Used or new battery grip

- At least 3 sources of lighting (for key, fill, and hair/back light)

- Diffusion for your lighting

- At least 2 C-stands, ideally 3 (if possible, one with a Rocky Mountain leg)

- A sandbag for each C-stand

- Shotgun mic to mount on your camera (or a dynamic hand mic with a cardioid pickup pattern, per Tom Schroeppel's preference, from *The Bare Bones Camera Course for Film and Video*)

- Zoom F1 field recorder or other recorder with boom mic

- Rode or other brand boom mic pole that's lightweight and telescopes to longer lengths

- Accessories for attaching the boom mic and field recorder to the boom pole (such as a Manfrotto metal thread and a shock absorber mount)

- An artificial fur and/or foam windscreen to reduce wind noise when recording sound outdoors

- An Auray or other brand cradle/stand for the boom pole, to attach to a C-stand

- 2 lav mics with recorders (such as Tascam)

- Batteries for all sound recording gear

- Atomos 5" or 7" or other brand and size monitor plus necessary accessories such as mount and cable(s) for connecting it to your camera

- Slate and erasable markers

Suggested Reading List

Save the Cat! and *Save the Cat! Goes to the Movies*, by Blake Snyder

How to Write a Movie in 21 Days, by Viki King

The Art of Dramatic Writing, by Lajos Egri

Film Scheduling, by Ralph S. Singleton

Film and Video Budgets 6 (sixth edition), by Maureen Ryan (I haven't yet read this book but while researching mine I came across persuasive endorsements of both the book and the author, so I'm including it here.)

Directing Actors - 25th Anniversary Edition: Creating Memorable Performances for Film and Television, by Judith Weston (There's an audio version featuring updated text from the original *Directing Actors* book on Audible, read by Weston.)

The Bare Bones Camera Course for Film and Video, by Tom Schroeppel and Chuck DeLaney (I cannot recommend this book enough.)

A Shot in the Dark: A Creative DIY Guide to Digital Video Lighting on (Almost) No Budget, by Jay Holben (Even if you only read the first several pages then decide to just suck it up and spend money on a few good lights, you will have gotten your money's worth!)

Rebel Without a Crew, by Robert Rodriguez

Independent Ed: What I Learned from My Career of Big Dreams, Little Movies, and the Twelve Best Days of My Life, by Edward Burns (A fantastic read that you will love.)

Cheap Movie Tricks: How to Shoot a Short Film for Under $2,000, by Rickey Bird (Another great book that covers the most important stuff.)

Feature Filmmaking at Used Car Prices, *Extreme DV*, and *The Miracle of Morgan's Cake: Production Secrets of a $15,000 Improv Sundance Feature* are all books by indie filmmaker Rick Schmidt (whose improvised movie, *Morgan's Cake*, went to Sundance in 1986).

Suggested Viewing List

Abigail's Party, written and directed by Mike Leigh

All That Jazz, written and directed by Bob Fosse

Another Day at the Office, written and directed by Richard Linklater (short film)

Before Sunrise, directed by Richard Linklater, written by Richard Linklater and Kim Krizan

Before Sunset, directed by Richard Linklater, written by Richard Linklater, Julie Delpy, and Ethan Hawke from a story by Linklater and Kim Krizan

Before Midnight, directed by Richard Linklater, written by Richard Linklater, Julie Delpy, and Ethan Hawke

The Brothers McMullen, written and directed by Edward Burns

Cold Turkey, directed by Norman Lear, written by Norman Lear and William Price Fox, Jr., based on the unpublished novel, *I'm Giving Them Up for Good* by Margaret and Neil Rau

Do the Right Thing, written and directed by Spike Lee

Eraserhead, written and directed by David Lynch

If Beale Street Could Talk, written and directed by Barry Jenkins, based on James Baldwin's novel

Metropolitan, written and directed by Whit Stillman

Morgan's Cake, written and directed by Rick Schmidt

Old Joy, written and directed by Kelly Reichardt, based on a short story by Jonathan Raymond

One Night in Miami…, directed by Regina King, written by Kemp Powers

"The Robert Rodriguez 10 Minute Film School (the first and original)," from Robert RodriguezHD on YouTube

Slacker, written and directed by Richard Linklater

Superstar: The Karen Carpenter Story, written and directed by Todd Haynes

Tampopo, written and directed by Juzo Itami

Tangerine, directed by Sean Baker, written by Sean Baker and Chris Bergoch

References

Books and Articles

Bird, Rickey. *Cheap Movie Tricks: How to Shoot a Short Film for Under $2,000*. Florida: Mango Publishing, 2017.

Egri, Lajos. *The Art of Dramatic Writing: Its Basis in the Creative Interpretation of Human Motives*. New York: Touchstone Books, 1972.

Friedman, Ron. *Decoding Greatness: How the Best in the World Reverse Engineer Success*. New York: Simon & Schuster, 2021.

Garrison, Tedric. "Shadows and Highlights: The Mark of Excellence," PictureCorrect, https://www.picturecorrect. com/shadows-highlights-black-white-photography/.

Holben, Jay. *A Shot in the Dark; A Creative DIY Guide to Digital Video Lighting on (Almost) No Budget*. Massachu- setts: Cengage Learning PTR, 2011.

King, Viki. *How to Write a Movie in 21 Days: The Inner Movie Method*. New York: Harper Paperbacks, 2020.

Murch, Walter. *In the Blink of an Eye: A Perspective on Filmmaking*. California: Silman-James Press, 2001.

Rodriguez, Robert. *Rebel without a Crew: Or How a 23-Year-Old Filmmaker with $7,000 Became a Hollywood Player*. Canada: Plume Press, 1996.

Ryan, Maureen. *Film and Video Budgets 6*. California: Michael Wiese Productions, 2015.

Schmidt, Rick. *Feature Filmmaking at Used-Car Prices: Second Revised Edition.* New York: Penguin Books, 2000.

Schmidt, Rick. *The Miracle of Morgan's Cake - Production Secrets of a $15,000 IMPROV Sundance Feature.*

Snyder, Blake. *Save the Cat! Goes to the Movies: The Screenwriter's Guide to Every Story Ever Told.* California: Michael Wiese Productions, 2007.

Snyder, Blake. *Save the Cat! The Last Book on Screenwriting You'll Ever Need.* California: Michael Wiese Productions, 2005.

Schroeppel, Tom, and Chuck DeLaney. *The Bare Bones Camera Course for Film and Video.* New York: Allworth Press, 2015.

Stutz, Phil, and Barry Michels. *The Tools: Five Tools to Help You Find Courage, Creativity, and Willpower--and Inspire You to Live Life in Forward Motion.* New York: Random House Publishing Group, 2013.

Taylor, David. *Digital Photography Complete Course: Learn Everything You Need to Know in 20 Weeks (DK Complete Courses).* New York: DK Publishing, 2015.

Weston, Judith. *Directing Actors - 25th Anniversary Edition: Creating Memorable Performances for Film and Television.* California: Michael Wiese Productions, 2021.

Singleton, Ralph S. *Film Scheduling: Or How Long Will It Take to Shoot Your Movie?* 2013.

Burns, Edward, and Todd Gold. *Independent Ed: Inside a Career of Big Dreams, Little Movies, and the Twelve Best Days of My Life.* New York: Avery Publishing, 2015.

Videos

"Audio is more important than video," from Vic Barry on YouTube.

"Cinematography Using Video Scopes / False Color, Waveform, Vectorscope," from SonduckFilm on YouTube.

"Ep 33 C-Stands," from Dave Donaldson on YouTube.

"Filmmaking Tips: Using Practical Lighting," from PremiumBeat for Shutterstock on YouTube.

"Ford v Ferrari Carroll Shelby speech," (from the movie *Ford v Ferrari*) on YouTube.

"How to Nail Exposure in Manual Mode" (for still photography but helpful for cinematography, too) from Sean Tucker on YouTube.

"Instantly improve your lighting with False Color," from The Film Look on YouTube.

"Introduction to Video Editing" and "Premiere Pro 2022 Essential Training" courses from Ashley Kennedy on LinkedIn Learning.

"Lessons for the No-Budget Feature" from Royal Ocean Film Society by Andrew Saladino on YouTube.

"Lighting 101: Direction of Light," from RocketJump Film School on YouTube.

"Massively Improve Your Audio with These 4 Effects in Premiere Pro," from Kevin Fremon on YouTube.

"Photography Tutorial: ISO, Aperture, Shutter Speed" (for still photography but helpful for cinematography) from Tek Syndicate by Ward Hale on YouTube.

"Pro Tip: How to set up a C-stand," from RocketJump Film School on YouTube.

"Roger Deakins on Learning to Light – Cinematography Techniques Ep. 1," on YouTube.

"Understanding Contrast Ratios," from Dale Snood for Vistek on YouTube.

Courtney Daniels is an independent filmmaker from Houston, Texas who lives in Los Angeles. She has written, directed and produced three feature films, *What Other Couples Do*, *Bedroom Story*, and *This Fucking Town*.

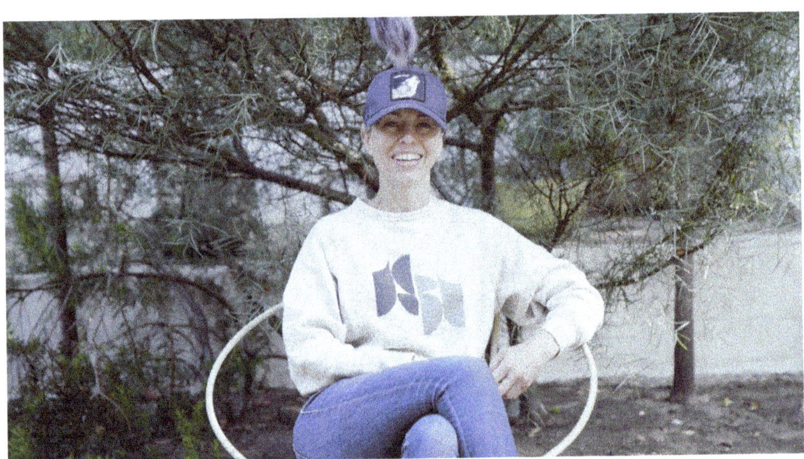